STARTING OVER

Reinventing Life After 60

PAT SKILLING KELLERMAN

www.reinventinglifeafter60.com

To order additional copies of this book, contact:
Xlibris Corporation
1-888-795-4274
www.Xlibris.com
Orders@Xlibris.com
21151

DEDICATION

This book is dedicated to
Frederic M. Hudson, Ph.D., whose words inspired me, and
to the kind men and women featured in this book who
shared their stories so that we might learn:

Adela Amador

Bob and Sally Ambrose

Stan Appelbaum

Donna Berg

Dick Bierly

Autry Brown

Richard Busch

Gene Clark

Betty and Jim Claypool

Evangeline Cothren

Beverley Cullen

Peggy Day

Jerry Engle

Bobby Enwright

Millie Finkel

Mary Ann Fontana

Peter and Mary Gregory

Charles Hamblin

Merwin Hans

Joanne Hobbs

Dick Hunter

Jake and Gwen Jolliff

Monty Justice

Steve Keiley

Rodney and Kathy Kling

Jeanette Kyllonen

Helen Lillich

Herb McKittrick

Sofie Minzel

Margaret More

Leo Neff

Mel Nowland

Ken Pasmanick

Malcolm Peplow

George Pucine

Dick Schiller

Mary Ann Schreit

Arnold Siegel

Tom and Mimi Skilling

Pat Smith

Jane Sprang

Maurice Steelman

Mike and Sue Turk

Bruce Valesco

Joe Walton

LeAnn Word

ACKNOWLEDGMENTS

Whenever I discuss *Starting Over* with someone new, the first question they ask is, "How did you find your stories?" I tell them about the many helpful folks around the country who suggested people they knew:

Harold Barrett, Judy Beaver, Nancy Blonowicz, Tom Cox, Bobby Enwright, Russ Groover, Dave Kellerman, Laura Kellerman, Steve Keiley, Sandy Knight, Jan Macidull, Marguerite Mitchell, Randy Philhours, Rose Plowchin, and Sue and Mike Turk;

Byron Crawford of the *Louisville Courier*, Joe Gerrety and Jeff Parrott of the *Lafayette Journal*, George Gill of the *Loudoun Times Mirror*, Ian Mylchreest of the *Las Vegas Review Journal*, Emily Toadvine of the *Danville Advocate Messenger*, and Melanie Burns of the *Jonesboro Sun*;

Suzanne Gilmore-Sakal of the Southwest Florida Seabird Sanctuary of Indian Shores, Florida; Kathy Failla of the International Executive Service Corps, Stamford, Connecticut; Ronna Metcalf of the Life Enrichment Senior Center, Tampa, Florida; Ann Remsen of Music for Minors, San Jose, California; Rosa Weinstein of Himmelfarb Mobile University, Rockville, Maryland; Sally Steele of the North Carolina Coastal

Federation, Newport, North Carolina; Don Reeves of the National Cowboy & Western Heritage Museum, Oklahoma City, Oklahoma; Roger Hand of RSVP, Santa Barbara, California and Barbara Tellefson of Unity Shoppe, Santa Barbara, California;

Thank you, one and all. This book came about because of your enthusiastic involvement.

Carol Deakman, Karen Groover, Jan Newcomb, Peggy Poe, and Greg Skilling provided special assistance. Thank you.

Jack Macidull, Kitty Rosati, Rose Rosetree, John Sullivan, and Sandra Young, published authors all, provided helpful insight and advice, as did my readers: Nancy Blonowicz, Linda Britt, Margaret Holland, and Laura Kellerman. Thank you for your feedback and encouragement.

CONTENTS

INTRODUCTION

"First, plan to live to be 100."

His words hung in the air. Frederic Hudson—sixty-six, tall, elegant, author, guru—stood in the middle of our large circle of participants. All of us were in California to attend "LifeLaunch", a four-day seminar at the Hudson Institute of Santa Barbara, to help us figure out where we wanted to go next with our lives. I'd been struggling with this for a couple of years. I was counting on Frederic to help me "launch" into something very big and important—my retirement.

My mind clicked away. Plan to live to be one hundred? That would change everything. I'd been thinking I had maybe fifteen to twenty more years left on this earth—living to age eighty or eighty-five. But Frederic was telling us to think bigger. I should be thinking more like thirty to thirty-five years. I'm sixty-five, and that would mean another career/another lifetime ahead of me!

Frederic is a developmental psychologist, and he was talking to us about life's psychological stages. He focused on the later years, from sixty and beyond, and was about to discuss people like me—people in their sixties.

"The sixties are about starting over," he began.

"Yesssss!" I thought. "That's just how I feel about my retirement. Soon I'll be able to start over and do whatever I want. Trouble is, I don't know what that is." I'd made up my mind not to retire unless I had something exciting out there to move toward. But I had no clue what that might be.

Frederic continued. "Find a role model ten years older than yourself." Now, how would I do that? When you're in your sixties and still in the workplace, you're the oldest thing around. I knew maybe two people in their seventies and eighties, and neither were women. The best role model I could think of who was leading the kind of active, vibrant life I hoped for was standing right in front of me, and he was neither retired nor ten years older.

Then it hit me—this is why I haven't been able to figure out what I want to do when I retire! I have no role models! Here I am, going to work everyday at AARP—a place where our entire focus is on the issues of those over age fifty—yet I have no role models for retirement in the twenty-first century. And a second later, it occurred to me that if I didn't have role models, most likely other people didn't have role models either.

The retired folks I saw while growing up led a much more sedentary life than I've envisioned—women in big aprons sitting in their rocking chairs on the porch, men sitting right there next to them. My grandmother retired from teaching. I remember her sewing, quilting and attending church meetings. My uncle moved to Florida and played golf. My father died too young to retire. My mother and the other women of my family were housewives and never 'retired' at all. I suspect my relatives weren't too different from others born in the early twentieth century.

Today, however, most of us are imagining something quite different. The old retirement picture doesn't work anymore. Our life expectancy is longer than that of our predecessors. We're healthier. Many of us are more affluent and better educated. We've traveled. Even the word "retirement" no longer fits, although we haven't coined a new word to replace it. With the Boomers retiring right behind us, those of us now in our sixties are on the cutting edge of a thirty-to-forty-year phenomena that will revolutionize "retirement." And few role models exist for us.

So there I was in Santa Barbara. It was November 2000. Frederic continued discussing life in our seventies, eighties and nineties—mentoring others, leaving a legacy, coming to terms with death. But I was thinking about living to one hundred and finding a role model.

Returning home a few days later, I began scanning the obituaries in my local newspaper. How old are the people in my town when they die? Was Frederic right? I discovered that about 85 percent of the residents in my community are in their eighties when they pass away. Fifteen years from now, when I enter my eighties, I reasoned, medical science will probably have made advances in extending life even further, into our nineties and beyond. Frederic was right. It was clear that I needed to rethink my future. In fact, all of us need to plan to live to be one hundred!

My quest to find a role model turned out to be simple, thanks to Frederic. He gave me the name of a woman who lives in my area. She's in her eighties. We meet for lunch and have a grand, old time talking about her life. I've learned from her. And along the way, I figured out what I wanted to do when I retired. I wanted to write a book about role models—all kinds of role models age sixty and beyond.

One criteria had to be that they were starting over, just as Frederic had said, doing new things with their lives. And whatever they were doing, it had to be something to which they were devoting a substantial amount of time, rather than an occasional pastime. Lastly, I wanted to find role models who were engaged in extending themselves to others. Research on aging clearly tells us that the happiest people are those involved in giving—being "other" focused. They also live the longest. My hope was that the stories of these over-sixty, involved, outward-focused men and women could inspire others to think creatively about their own journey starting over.

This book is about what to do, and how to begin. It contains stories of "retired" men and women from across the United States. They were once executives, teachers, accountants, salesmen, military men, entrepreneurs and homemakers. Many are working harder than they ever worked before, and loving every minute of it, because it's their own personal adventure. They are leading passionate lives. Some are fulfilling dreams they've had forever; some took a slight detour from what they were doing before retirement; others stumbled onto something totally new. All believe their "retirement" lifestyle keeps them vital and alive. None of them is interested in the rocking chair.

I traveled around the country in my own brand new "starting over" interviewing these delightful, busy people. Each chapter contains one of their stories. You'll learn about the catalyst prompting their adventure, and what their new lives involve. They share advice in case you'd like to do something similar. And they talk about retirement. You'll receive maximum benefit from this book by reading each and every story, whether or not a particular topic may seem in line with your interests. It's the *collective* wisdom and advice found in these forty tales that will give you the greatest food for thought and most expand your perspective as you contemplate your own retirement.

Starting Over's conclusion summarizes the themes found within the stories and offers four critical steps to follow as you prepare to start over. Also included are the key questions all retirees need to ask themselves—not just before leaving the workplace, but from time to time through the years.

As you read these brief chapters, I hope you'll begin to see possibilities for your own starting over. One story is about a long-time friend of mine, Dick Hunter, age eighty-seven. A full-time volunteer for twenty years, every morning Dick puts on a coat and tie and heads to a place he loves. I asked him once what made his volunteer work so worthwhile. He replied,

"For all my senior years I've had the extreme pleasure each day of looking forward, instead of looking back." That inspires me. These stories of *Starting Over* inspire me. I hope they'll inspire you, too.

PK
Leesburg, Virginia
November 2001

*We must be willing to get rid of the life we planned,
so as to have the life that is waiting for us.*

Joseph Campbell
Reflections on the Art of Living

OKLAHOMA UPGRADES

Just imagine. You have personally refurbished and upgraded over six thousand computers and donated them to the Oklahoma City Public Schools and other non-profit organizations! That's the story of Mel Nowland, sixty-eight, and Gene Clark, seventy-five, retired engineers of Oklahoma City, Oklahoma. They're brothers-in-law. They didn't know a thing about fixing computers until they started fiddling around with them.

"It was a learning process," Mel said, as the three of us sat in their workroom and he explained how it all began. "Neither Gene nor I had worked with computers previously. But a few years ago, the Easter Seals Foundation needed some, so I thought I'd see if I could rebuild one to give to them. My wife, Vera, has been disabled with childhood rheumatoid arthritis since she was twenty-eight, so our relationship with Easter Seals goes back a long way.

"Initially, I got computers from AT&T. I'm retired from AT&T and knew about their surplus computer program. I started tinkering and it didn't take long before I figured out the inner workings of them. I ended up refurbishing three for Easter Seals.

"Before long, Easter Seals folks told people in other agencies, and that's how it started. Eight years ago or so, computers were expensive. It would have been impossible for many of the smaller non-profits to purchase them.

"When Gene retired a couple years later, he announced that he wanted to work on computers, too. Nowadays, Gene actually upgrades more computers than I."

"I get here about ten thirty and stay until five thirty or six," Gene said. "We've taken over this room in Mel's house and work here at our benches every day. Mel's our spokesperson. He has all the contacts and knows who to talk to in the various state agencies and school boards.

"Three or four years into our work, we decided we needed to affiliate with a 501(c)3 charitable organization so that computer donations could be tax deductible. We didn't want to be a 501(c)3 ourselves because of all the paperwork required, but we did want to find an existing organization that would sponsor us. We found AMBUCS, a service organization dedicated to creating independence and opportunities for people with disabilities. AMBUCS gives computers mostly to disabled children and we helped them get started. In fact, we still help them."

"We've had some neat experiences," Mel said. "Through the Oklahoma City PC Users Group we provided 114 computers to medical schools in Africa. The users group got Feed the Children, which is based here in Oklahoma City, to haul the computers to Charleston Air Force Base in South Carolina. The Air Force flew them to Africa to be distributed by UNESCO.

"There's a local missionary who works in town as a handyman until he gets enough money to pay for airfare back to Haiti, and he takes some of our computers back with him. Other missionaries have taken them to Guam and the Philippines."

Gene added, "The computers we deliver to grade schools are equipped with shareware programs suitable for students pre-kindergarten to seventh grade. Most of them are games. There's a teacher at one of our middle schools who's teaching kids how to fix computers at recess and during their lunch break. We furnished him with a lot of computers, at first.

"Those kids are doing such a great job they're actually working on computers for other schools now, and the teacher sometimes helps us."

"Soon we won't have a job anymore," Mel quipped.

"We've had wonderful publicity," he continued. "Reporters from the *Daily Oklahoman* have helped us a lot. Every time we get low on old computers, they've written a story. Right now my entire garage is packed to the ceiling with computers as a result of the last one. My car hasn't had a home for years."

Besides their computer work, Mel and Gene also work on telethons for Jerry Lewis' Muscular Dystrophy Association event, the Children's Miracle Network, the Arthritis Foundation, the Leukemia Foundation, etc. "This September we'll do our 111th telethon! Unbelievable, huh?" Gene remarked. "We set up the telephones that you see the volunteers using during broadcasts, and the light boards that flash and tote boards displaying the rolling dollar pledges. We get lots of people to help us. We helped raise a million dollars during the last one, over fifty million in all, and working on these shows is a nice change of pace."

Advice to others who'd like to upgrade computers?

1. Find a few computers to get yourself started. Then let your newspaper know so they can do a story.
2. You'll need a place to store your computers. And a place to work. We've never rented a spot. We've always just borrowed a room from here and there.
3. Get your components from the computers you discard.
4. Align with other organizations so you don't have to form your own 501(c)3. They provide assistance, too. AMBUCS prints our brochures.

"And we'll be glad to help anyone around the country who wants to do this," Mel said, smiling. "We give a three-minute soldering course and a five-minute course on everything you need to know about electronics."

"Why do you do this?" I asked.

"I'm probably working harder now than I did when I was employed," Gene replied. "I guess the gratification of helping others is what keeps me going. I live by myself—been married three times and have five kids. It's an outlet for conversation and physical contact. You've got to keep your mind and body active, or you're just going to wither away and die. I guess it's a matter of self-preservation."

"Vera and I can't travel," Mel said. "I have to be doing something or I'd go crazy. I have rheumatoid arthritis, too. I'm probably the only guy you've ever met who got rheumatoid arthritis from sleeping with someone," he joked. "Seriously, I'm in pain all the time. Being busy keeps my mind off my pain. Years ago, when Vera was first diagnosed, the children were five and two and a half years old. I couldn't see how I could deal with it all. The tunnel was long and with no end. I learned then that keeping my mind active was the best medicine. Nowadays, I get around with a three-wheel cart when I leave the house to go grocery shopping or whatever. Mental stimulation is essential if I want to have a life."

"What would you tell others about to retire?" I asked them both.

Mel replied first. "They can sit down and rest and die young, or they can get on with it," he said. "Find something. We found a need with Easter Seals and filled it. You can't sit at home to find the needs. You've got to get out and volunteer someplace."

Gene added, "If you didn't like what you did for a living, do something else. The Retired and Senior Volunteer Program (RSVP) is a good place to start. AARP also. Or AT&T's Telephone Pioneers. We built seven hundred peeping Easter eggs to be used in Easter egg hunts for blind children. And we've made carnival games for the Muscular Dystrophy Association. Now the police department wants some of our games, too."

Mel summed up their philosophy nicely. "We enjoy what we do. You will, too, once you get into it. You'll be glad you got involved with others. You'll never know joy like the joy of giving. It has brought meaning and purpose to all that we do."

PEGGY JEAN'S PIES

"We sat around Jean's kitchen table one night trying to come up with brilliant ideas for a business we might operate together. Finally, Jean said, 'We could always sell my marvelous apple pies!'"

Peggy Day, seventy-six, of Columbia, Missouri, was explaining how she and her partner started their business. "We had eight hundred dollars between us. We bought a used refrigerator and began looking for a place to rent that could pass city health inspections. We finally found a little house down behind a used-car lot—not the best section of town. Everybody tried to scare us to death about the risks we were taking, but in March 1994, when I was sixty-eight, we opened our business.

"The local paper is always doing articles on new businesses, so we called the business columnist and he came out and did a story on us. When the food editor learned of it, she did a whole front page piece in the food section."

That was all the advertising they needed. "Peggy Jean's Pies" became famous overnight. Before the articles, they'd been driving around, selling pies to restaurants out of their cars. But after that publicity, they decided to sell to the public. They took phone orders for pick-ups a few days later. "The first time we had to have ten pies ready at once we weren't sure we'd be able to do it. But we did it, and it got easier over time.

"Our location was atrocious and a year after we opened, we moved downtown. It was a much bigger place and we got the lunch crowd. We started baking baby pies instead of selling slices. They sold very well. But customers wanted us to make sandwiches, too, so that they could come for lunch. So we began offering a limited menu—one quiche, one soup, five kinds of sandwiches, and pie, of course. People liked that. We worked like crazy but it was fun and we did very well."

Five years later, when their landlord wanted to significantly raise the rent, Peggy and Jean decided to move. They found a place in the suburbs and had the restaurant configured to their specifications. Their new place is furnished with antiques, and has balcony rooms for parties and meetings. "For the first time, we took out a loan from the bank. That was scary.

"Now that we have a big operation, we're open six days a week for breakfast and lunch. We've expanded our menu— more soup, more quiche, more sandwiches, salads, and thirty different kinds of pies. For breakfast, we serve a full breakfast menu. Now we have twenty-one full- and part-time employees. The restaurant's unique, so tour buses come here on their way to Iowa or wherever. Business is good."

Peggy and her partner have developed a nice mail-order business with the pies. Special packaging keeps them intact during shipping. They have attractive gift wrap, and guarantee two-day delivery. Every Tuesday, pies go out to all over the U.S.

Just inside the front door of the restaurant hangs the plaque given to them in 1996 when they were designated Columbia's Small Business of the Year. Laminated plaques hang nearby displaying the articles about Peggy Jean's Pies featured in *Southern Living* magazine in 1999, and *Victoria* magazine in 2001.

"We've been told so many times what an inspiration we are to others, I guess because we'd never done anything like this before, and we just went out and did it. Various groups around town have asked us to do seminars about starting a business. We always ask our audience the same question: 'Are you ready to have a baby?'

"We've had inquiries about franchising—I don't know if we'll do that. Nothing stays the same, so we'll have new products. We're now selling unbaked pie crust and as soon as we get the packaging figured out, we're going to start selling the filling. We'll be looking at anything new in packaging."

Peggy offers the following advice to others who might like to start a food business:

1. Start small and don't get in too big a hurry. It takes time.
2. Call your local newspaper. Let people know.
3. Whatever your product, be consistent. I want to hear today's customers say that it tastes just the same as the first pie they tasted.
4. It's easy to get in a rut, so if you want to grow, you must take chances.
5. You win some, you lose some. I go a lot on my gut feeling when making decisions.

"We do still have problems once in awhile because we're women. When we got ready to borrow money for our new place, we were turned down by the first bank we approached. The loan officer said, 'You're two women, and you're just a little old.' Oh my," said Peggy, shaking her head. "We could have made their lives miserable had we chosen.

"When we opened our first place, a man came in and asked to see the owner. I said, 'You're looking at her.' He replied, 'No, not the help—I want the owner.' I pointed beyond him and asked, 'See that door?' He left. A couple of years later, the same man came into our place downtown. He was halfway across the floor before he saw me. Without blinking an eye, he turned on his heel and walked right back out that door! Guess he didn't realize we'd moved," Peggy said, laughing.

Retirement isn't on Peggy's mind very often. "By the time I get home at six or seven at night, I'm tired. I've been at the restaurant since nine thirty in the morning. I've been working on shipping orders, returning phone calls, taking reservations. I wait on people, run errands, and take care of employee needs. Then I go home to my husband. We've been married fifty-four years.

"Everyone should have something to focus on," she continued. "I was a homemaker until my children finished college. I went to work when I was fifty-six, selling real estate. Then I left that to work in the bank. That's where Jean and I met and became friends. When we started this business, she was forty and I was sixty-eight. So it doesn't matter how old you are. You just need to find something to do that you really love—something you love so much that you don't mind being tired because you're so involved in it.

"I love my life," Peggy said, wrapping up our talk. "You know what's so exciting? Here, I'm not my husband's wife, or my children's mother, or someone's grandmother. I'm me. This business is for me."

"I'm so proud! So proud!"

FOOTBALL'S THE THING

After thirty-five years in the NFL, Joe Walton was ready for a change. Like his father before him, Joe had graduated from the University of Pittsburgh and been drafted to play for the Washington Redskins. He went on to play for the New York Giants, later coaching for them and then returning to coach for Washington. Moving back to New York to become head coach for the Jets, Joe finished his career in the NFL with the Pittsburgh Steelers.

"Most people don't realize the long hours coaches work in professional football," said Joe. "You're with the players from nine to five, and at night you prepare for the games. Normally, I didn't get home until eleven. On Saturdays, we'd practice in the morning, work on the playbook in the afternoon, have dinner with the players at six, and more meetings in the evening. And then of course, there's the game on Sunday.

"That was just during the season," Joe continued. "Training camp starts in July and the regular season continues to January. Right after that, the draft begins. And then mini-camps. It's a grueling schedule and I was ready for a change. So when Chuck Noll retired, I decided it was time for me to retire, too."

The job with the Steelers meant returning to Beaver Falls, Pennsylvania, where Joe had grown up and where he wanted to retire. When he left the Steelers, he did a little banquet speaking, and played golf. He loved having more time for family and friends. But he missed the challenge of his old career, and missed teaching. "You get the disease," he confided.

Joe's cousin was coaching at Slippery Rock, and a friend was coaching at another small college. Joe wondered about something like that for himself. As luck would have it, Robert Morris College, only twenty-five minutes from Beaver Falls, was looking for someone to start a football program for the school.

Joe was intrigued with the idea of building a complete program from scratch. "The NFL is very specialized; no one has the whole picture, or works outside their niche," he said. "I figured just working within the budget of a small college would be a challenge," he said, laughing. And Joe had never worked with young people. The college gave him a year to prepare.

His first office on campus was a windowless room containing a desk and telephone. He had nothing else—no practice fields, no locker room, no game field, no uniforms. Joe hired Dan Radakovich as assistant coach, an NFL friend who had coached at Penn State.

"For the first week or so we sat around strategizing," Joe said. "We decided we were going to teach our players everything we taught in the NFL. Our playbook is exactly the same as my Jets playbook. Granted, we'd have to go slower; our players are full-time students, not full-time professional athletes.

"We watched the recruiting films of other small colleges, and visited them to learn about their football programs. They had tiny locker rooms, tiny training rooms, and were playing on old softball or soccer fields. Ours wasn't the only program without money," Joe mused.

Joe and Dan built a program for sixty players—a reasonable size for a small college. Friends helped them out. A college buddy who owned a construction company in Pittsburgh agreed to build the locker room for practically nothing. A former equipment manager for the Steelers helped them find equipment. They negotiated to rent the local high school's field for their games.

"We had planned a program for sixty players, purchased for sixty players, and when the program started a year later, 145 kids showed up! But we never turn anyone away. Gradually, the numbers are winnowed down. Players drop out because they aren't getting the play time they'd imagined, or because their grades are suffering, or their schedule is too full."

Robert Morris College is now a university. Five years after the football program began, the school was division champion, and again, the following year. This year they're doing great as well.

Joe says he has the ideal life. We sat in his large, window-filled office, watching their recruiting film. "Colleges hold 'Recruiting Nights' at motels around the country. Twenty-five to thirty high school coaches come to the motel to show newspaper clippings and films of their star players to the college coaches. We call the players who interest us and try to recruit them. We hope to get eighty new kids each year."

"What's it like working with young people?" I asked.

"They're great," Joe replied. "They're eager. They want to learn. They practice well. They have no pre-conceived notions. They're trying to find themselves. You try to instill in them what life's all about and what football is all about. A lot of what I do is counseling.

"I had to change my style. I have to repeat more, go slower. I believe in fundamentals and discipline. But I also believe they've got to have fun. The kids like using the professional plays, and get a kick out of seeing their plays on television during NFL games. And I think they like having coaches from the NFL."

A few years ago, Joe decided to hold a celebrity golf tournament to raise money for the program. "People pay to play with celebrities, and now we are also getting corporate sponsors. It's been a life-saver. The tournament is held in May and we spend March and April getting ready. Each year we've cleared $40,000-$50,000 for the football program. It's a lot of work and a lot of fun. After that I play golf and get ready for training camp."

What advice would Joe give others who want to apply the experience and knowledge of their careers in a smaller environment? "Well, I'd tell them not to take shortcuts," Joe replied instantly. "Don't try to simplify everything just because it's a smaller arena. Don't cheat people. Don't waste all you know. And make sure you enjoy whatever you do. Another thing to remember—wherever you've been, you've made a lot of friends. Don't be afraid to ask for help. Most are glad to offer a hand."

What are Joe's thoughts on retirement? "I don't consider myself retired," he replied. "I'm in my mid-sixties and I look forward to it all. I like the college, I like the people. I like being home every night in time for dinner. Every January and February, my wife and I go to Puerto Rico. We've been going for years and have good friends there. We have family and good friends here, too. I'll stay in this job as long as I'm having a good time and the college still wants me. It's a great life!"

Joe Walton is a happy man.

FOR THE BIRDS

Beyond the huge, sliding glass doors leading to the balcony of Pat Smith's condominium was the water, the palm trees and bushes on the far bank, a mangrove island off to the right. Below her balcony on the Little McPherson Bayou in Pass-a-Grille, Florida, sailboats rocked gently in their moorings, and pelicans sat atop every piling.

"That's how I got started," Pat explained, as we sat in her living room looking out over the water. "I saw a pelican struggling on one of the low branches of that tree over there, and figured he must not be able to fly. So I called the Seabird Sanctuary on Redlington Shores. They came quickly by boat and rescued the poor thing. A month or so later I saw a cormorant caught in a fishing line, and called the sanctuary again. I was so impressed by their quick response, and the challenge of helping these injured, frightened birds that I decided to sign up."

The Suncoast Seabird Sanctuary usually cares for about six hundred birds at any given time: pelicans, great blue herons, egrets, cormorants, and ducks. All are being nursed back to health. Most will be well enough to be returned to the wild.

"I started out feeding baby birds born at the sanctuary," Pat said, "and learning about the hundreds of calls we get each year about fledgling birds falling out of the nest. People are afraid to pick them up because they've heard the old wives' tale that babies will be abandoned by their parents if they're handled by humans. It's not true. So we encourage people to find the nest and put the babies back. Or if the nest is destroyed or unreachable, we'll tell them how to make a substitute nest, line it with leaves and grass, and hang it back in the tree.

"I was still employed then, sixty-nine, divorced, my children were grown and gone, and I'd planned to work forever. But I was falling in love with bird work and I wanted to be a rescuer. To do that, I'd have to be on call and available. So I retired, and that's when I really got involved."

Four days a week, Pat is on "dispatch" with the sanctuary. When calls come in from concerned citizens, Pat heads out to the designated locations. "One call may be from lower St. Petersburg, another may come from North Tampa, another is on the Gulf Beaches, and so on. I spend most of my time driving. Last year, I put over twenty-eight thousand miles on my van just rescuing birds. On days that I'm not on dispatch, I often get calls from other rescuers who need help. We keep in touch with each other and with the sanctuary by cell phone."

In between the cages, large and small, in the back of Pat's van, are long-handled nets, tree trimming shears and assorted useful tools. She has a sixteen-feet extension ladder for tree rescues.

"Many seabirds get fishhooks in their beaks, wings or feet. Fishing line trails from the hook and these lines get tangled in tree branches or caught on pilings. If not spotted and rescued, the birds would starve to death. Injured birds are distressed and panic when approached by a human. Rescuing requires training, practice, and patience.

"I love knowing I'm saving these birds, and I like the physicality often required on rescues. You have to run pretty fast to catch a seagull. I've often wondered what people think when they see this gray-haired, old lady running across their lawn," Pat said, laughing. "I feel good about being able to do something like this at age seventy-two.

"Pelicans are easier to catch. When they're hungry, which is most of the time, they'll come right up to you if you have a fish. When I drop the fish in front of them, I grab their beak when they reach for it. Then I carefully fold their wings, put the bird under my arm and carry it to a cage."

Pat says all kinds of rescue efforts go on daily around the country. In Florida, many people get involved in rescuing baby turtles. To learn more about rescue work, she suggests readers call the sanctuaries, shelters and volunteer groups in their area to see what jobs are available. There's usually no pay or reimbursement for expenses involved in volunteer rescue work. Rescue efforts for the Seabird Sanctuary have required some investment—she bought her own nets, binoculars, ladder and tree trimmers—but not all volunteer work requires that. You never know until you check.

Pat will continue to rescue birds as long as she's able. "As another transplanted northerner, I feel a certain responsibility for the continuing destruction of the habitats of these beautiful creatures. Ninety percent of their injuries are caused by humans."

I wondered aloud how Pat liked retirement now that she'd actually done it.

"I never intended to retire. I enjoyed my work, and I'd done a lot of research about retirement some years ago. Many people look forward to it all their lives, but their plans don't always work out. They make drastic changes like moving to Florida or Arizona but find their new environment is not what they'd hoped for. They retire *from* something, not *to* something.

"No matter where you live, the most important thing is that you're involved in something that makes you want to get up in the morning. Just to quit working does not fulfill the human spirit.

"One day last week I had seven rescues: three pelicans, a baby dove, a sea gull, a loon, and a muscovy duck. As I drove away from the sanctuary that evening and headed home, I was exhilarated. The birds were safe. It was a good day's work."

THE WHITE COATS
ARE COMING!

Three hundred men and women comprise the Sun City Center, Florida Emergency Squad—the only all-volunteer emergency squad in the nation receiving no government funding. And all the volunteers are seniors.

"The people who move to Sun City are people who want to be involved—they want to connect," said Jeanette Kyllonen. Divorced, a homemaker, mother of four, and equestrian from Minnesota, Jeanette's partner died shortly after they moved to Florida. "I was sixty-five, alone, and wanted something to do. Now I'm an EMT," she said proudly.

Jerry Engle, eighty-one, is a retired Navy captain. "I commanded four ships in three wars," said Jerry. "I figured I ought to be able to drive an ambulance. Originally, that was my plan. I'm still a driver and get recertified for that once a year. But I ended up becoming an EMT, too. It's immensely satisfying."

Herb McKittrick, seventy-six, was at a party and overheard a team captain from the squad talking about the work he was doing. "His enthusiasm was contagious. He loved helping people and being part of the close community of volunteers," said Herb. "That was good enough for me. I was a widower with time on my hands." Herb became an EMT and is now chief of the emergency squad.

Becoming an Emergency Medical Technician (EMT) is not for the faint of heart. It's a long process. "You might as well figure on giving up five months of your life while you're going to school," said Jeanette. "A neighbor and I decided to take the training together. Thank heavens, because we studied together, quizzed each other, and urged each other on when one or the other of us would get discouraged about all the memorization involved."

Jerry continued. "Hillsborough County Community College offers a 120-hour curriculum in emergency medicine. We went to classes three hours a day, twice a week, to learn about anatomy, patient assessment, the respiratory system, the circulatory system, basic life support, legal responsibilities, personal safety, and so on. Learning *how to do it* is another matter. Our practical training was another twelve hours a week for six weeks."

"And we were studying all the rest of the time," added Herb, "so that it all sunk in and we'd be ready to pass the certification exam."

"Our emergency squad made over twelve thousand ambulance runs last year," said Jerry. To provide this twenty-four-hour service to their community of fifteen thousand people, every ambulance carries a team of three—the first responder who can provide advanced first aid, the driver, and the EMT who heads the team. Volunteers are organized in teams of twenty-five. The emergency squad has eight teams, with each team on duty every eight days for a twenty-four-hour period. "Our team made over one hundred ambulance runs last month," said Jerry.

"We also have wheelchair vans that we use to transport people to dialysis or other non-emergency appointments," Herb added. "And there's no charge for any of our services."

While on duty, the team hangs out in the Ready Room, all dressed in the white jackets of the squad. Some are talking quietly, some are reading the newspaper or playing cards, some are snoozing. But when a call comes in, the dispatcher broadcasts it on the loudspeaker and everyone stops what they're doing and listens. Simultaneously, a television screen in the Ready Room displays the address of the caller. The next team of three is gone in a flash.

Three years ago, Herb supported the first female candidate to run for emergency squad chief. When she won, she asked Herb to be her assistant chief of purchasing. His job was to purchase supplies for the squad, take care of the physical plant, and oversee vehicle and equipment repairs. When the chief's two-year term was over, the nominating committee asked Herb if he would run for the job.

Herb has been chief for a year. "This is my life now," he said. "For four years, I've been here for a portion of just about every day. I love it. I schedule refresher classes for the squad with our director of education, and oversee many other things going on here. I'm also out in the community, talking with people who are in charge of nursing homes or assisted living communities, making sure they are aware of what we do. I meet with members of the security patrol. And I'm making sure we stay within state compliance."

"A portion of each day I spend in the Ready Room, just listening. But I'm an EMT first," Herb emphasized. "I work on two teams. My term as chief will be over at the end of this year. I'll be on the Board for one year after my term is up. And I'll stay on my teams for at least two more years until my new wife retires."

"You have to be strong, quick, and knowledgeable to do this work," I asserted. "Isn't it stressful and demanding?"

"It can be," Jerry replied. "The very first ambulance run I went on was a suicide, a gunshot to the head. But most aren't like that."

"And you get more comfortable, the more runs you do," added Jeanette.

"Generally, we don't deal with life-and-death situations," said Herb. "The advanced life support paramedics in town handle patients who are unconscious, having a seizure, chest pains, a stroke, or difficulty breathing. Nevertheless, EMTs must pass a recertification exam every two years."

What advice would this team of go-getters give to others who'd like to be EMTs? "You don't need to start as an EMT," Jerry said.

"Yes," Jeanette added, "Initially, I went through the first responder advanced first aid training, and then later went on to more advanced training. That way you get to see if you like doing this work before you commit to five months of EMT training."

"We're on duty twenty-four hours at a time, every eight days," added Jerry. "So the job actually consumes most of two days by the time you've rested from your night duty. You need to be prepared to spend that amount of time."

Why do they do this? "You're doing something worthwhile with your life," said Jeanette. "You're not sitting around twiddling your thumbs."

"And it's such a good feeling to be able to help people," Herb added. "I wonder why I never helped people earlier. I take every single day as a gift. When you hold someone's hand who's shaking and scared, and help to calm them as we speed to the hospital, that makes that day worthwhile."

"And the fellowship and camaraderie among our team members is very special, too," Jerry said.

Jeanette laughed when I asked her what she thought about retirement.

"Retirement? What's that?" she asked. "Living in a retirement village takes a lot of time and energy! I never played before. This life is so much fun."

"The variety has been the fun of it," said Jerry. "My wife, Shirley, and I have done everything from working part-time at Disney World, to taking motor-home trips, to clubs. Shirley's an artist. I'm an EMT. We enjoy it all."

Herb said, "I hope people look forward to retirement with great anticipation and jump into whatever really stirs their hearts, full bore. Find a passion. We're only given a short time on this earth. We need to live that time with gusto!"

The average age at the emergency squad is seventy-two.

THE TREE LADY
OF WEST LAFAYETTE

In a god-awful, beat up, old junk heap of a pick-up truck, Helen Lillich, seventy-eight, is seen daily making the rounds in West Lafayette, Indiana.

"It started with letters to the editor," she said. "That's a good way to get people stirred up. I asked if anyone was interested in a cleaner, greener town. A couple of people responded. Then I went to the mayor, whom I knew, and told her I wanted to be involved in sprucing up West Lafayette. Another woman wrote to the mayor and suggested tree planting to beautify a parkway." Helen called her, and Piroska Haywood and Helen have been *partners in crime* ever since.

"We wrote other letters to the editor asking readers, 'Would you be willing to donate twenty-five dollars a year to plant trees along Sagamore Parkway?' We received one hundred dollars in the mail, our husbands donated twenty-five dollars each, and we got thirty other people we knew to each contribute twenty-five dollars.

"With nine hundred dollars, we purchased fifty-five hockberry trees," said Helen. "We thought we'd conquered the world. We gave volunteers plastic milk jugs and asked them to be responsible for watering two or three trees a week.

"And anytime there was anything noteworthy going on in town that had a link to what we were doing, we'd write another letter to the editor.

"After that we started a mail fundraising campaign. We wrote to all the doctors, lawyers, dentists and ministers listed in the phone book. There were about two hundred of them, and we got back four thousand dollars. With that kind of support, we were able to have two plantings that year.

"I started doing this while I was still working. Then when I retired from teaching high school English at sixty-five, things really started happening.

"The mayor hired me to 'do whatever I thought was necessary to beautify the town.' At first we focused on picking up trash. The courts assigned people who had to do twenty to thirty hours of community service to pick up trash for us. Then I'd transport it to the dump in my truck."

For several years, Helen and her partner aimed at planting one hundred new trees each year. Then they noticed the old, cracked asphalt median strips on several of their streets and boulevards. "That turned out to be a huge undertaking," Helen said. "Once the asphalt was removed, we put in soil.

"There's no such thing as dirt cheap," she remarked, laughing. "Dirt is expensive. Our largest median is fourteen feet wide and five hundred feet long. It cost thirty-six hundred dollars for the dirt alone! We wanted the dirt to be rounded off into mounds so that the landscaping could be seen by people driving by.

"There are lots of things to consider when planting by roadways. All the trees and plants have to be tolerant to fumes and the salt put down on the streets in the winter. For that reason, we used juniper trees, bayberry bushes and rugosa roses. The city has installed an underground watering pipeline for us, but soaker hoses need to be put down in the spring and taken up in the fall. And all our landscaping projects require a tremendous amount of mulching, weeding, spraying and trash pick-up."

As Helen and I bumped along in her pick-up truck past one landscaping project to the next, she said, "Planting trees is an ongoing process. We plant about one hundred replacement trees each year. As old trees are dying and coming down, new ones need to be planted. And trees are knocked down all the time by cars, believe it or not." Having now planted three thousand trees, the focus of the West Lafayette Tree Fund, as they've come to be called, is maintenance. The city has hired someone to pick up trash, as well as a part-time, seventy-year-old assistant to Helen and Piroska because their projects have gotten so big.

Arriving back at Helen's gracious, antique-filled home, she reflected on what advice she'd give to others interested in community projects. "Here's my advice," she remarked:

1. Find a soul-mate—someone else who feels as strongly as you do.
2. Prepare for disappointment—people will let you down like crazy.
3. Pick something that's in style. Greening is in style, and that has helped enormously.
4. Personally acknowledge financial contributions. Every time I get a check, I call the individual and thank them. They ask questions and offer lots of great suggestions. And I try to keep up with these calls day by day.
5. I read the paper and if I see the name of anyone I think would be interested, or if I meet them at parties, I put them on our mailing list.

"What are your thoughts on retirement?" I asked.

"I think most people fritter their time away. I read someplace everyone needs something to do that really needs doing," Helen replied. "I think you doggone well better have lined up something you want to do when you retire. Otherwise, it gets pretty dull. You just get lazier and lazier.

"I'm not as driven as I used to be," Helen concluded. "But I think I'm still driven to be worthwhile and responsible. I've always been goal-oriented. Retirement without goals would be incredibly boring, don't you think? And it sure wouldn't be any fun. Something to do that really needs doing can be challenging and enjoyable, and give purpose to each new day."

RICHARD'S
MAGNIFICENT
OBSESSION

Richard Busch is one of those lucky people who has a passion—something they love so much that they must do it, that to not do it would be a form of dying. "But it's not just a passion for me," he said. "It's an obsession."

Richard was editor-in-chief of *National Geographic's Traveler* magazine. He had been involved with writing, editing, and photography his entire thirty-year career. He and his wife, Olwen, a freelance author and public relations consultant, lived in the Virginia suburbs of Washington, DC. When a neighbor mentioned a class she was taking at the local community center, Richard thought it sounded interesting, so he signed up. Instantly, he was hooked.

The class was pottery, and it met once a week for three hours.

Richard spent every spare moment at the studio, often logging as many as twelve hours weekly. "It was all about the joy of making something beautiful," he said, "forming a shape from soft clay, decorating it, and seeing it come out of the kiln as a piece of useable stoneware." His teacher encouraged him and told him he had talent.

Ignited by his newfound passion for potting, Richard got his own wheel and kiln after two years of lessons so that he could pursue pottery at home, as well as at the community center. To further his education, he attended weekend workshops of well-known potters, joined potters' organizations, and subscribed to half a dozen ceramics magazines.

Richard began selling some of his pieces in craft shows around the area. For two years in a row, he sold over $2,000 worth of pots. "With that modest bit of success, I began to think about the possibility of making this a second career," he recalled. "I'd been a professional journalist for three decades, and had achieved a fair measure of success. But I couldn't see myself continuing that much longer. I'd 'been there, done that.' My passion for potting was soaring, and I couldn't escape the thought of making a major change in my life.

"So I started thinking about retiring, building a large kiln, and setting up a proper studio and showroom. The dilemma, of course, was both financial and physical. With a daughter still in college, could I afford to leave my job? At the same time I understood that potting is physical. If I were going to do this, I'd need to do it fairly soon while I still had the energy and drive.

"My wife and I talked to our financial planner to see if there was any way this dream might be possible. When he said we'd probably be okay if I retired early, we started looking for a place in the country—a place that would have the space for me to build a kiln, set up a studio and a showroom, and launch a business. In our wildest dreams, we never imagined *this*!"

Down a country road, a few miles west of Leesburg, Virginia is *"this"*—a converted barn sitting on twenty acres of lovely, rolling open land and woods. It is twenty-five miles from their former home, but oh, so far from their former life. The barn sits on a hillside with entrances on both levels. Their home is on the top level, in what was once a huge open loft—rough-hewn rafters above, large picture windows open to the fields beyond.

Down a slope and around the back of the barn are the entrances to the first floor, the former stables where Richard has his bright 48'x22' studio and a separate 20'x20' showroom. Huge windows open to views of birds, deer, and the countryside. Not far from the barn is a cottage—the former tenant's house, which they rent for income. Happily, the rent from the cottage pays for more than half of their mortgage and taxes—a big help to a new business.

So what does having a pottery business entail? It varies. "One day, I might be throwing pots all day," said Richard. "The clay has to stiffen before it can be trimmed. Then the next day I'll trim them, or put texture patterns on the pieces. Next comes the bisque firing in an electric kiln, and then all the pieces are glazed and loaded into the big propane-fueled kiln for a fifteen-hour glaze firing. It's a lot of physical work, but I really love it."

Of course, the business is much more than making and firing pots. Richard spends at least as much time marketing: making contacts, extending his network, entering competitions, writing letters and approaching galleries about displaying his pots (he is currently represented by five galleries around the country), developing a mailing list for publicizing his twice-a-year weekend studio sales that draw hundreds of people, and other business-related matters. Joining the Loudoun County Visitors and Convention Association has helped him promote his work in the area. And he's been profiled in local newspapers.

Richard is obviously delighted with his new life. "I love getting up in the morning and going down to my studio and working away, creating beautiful objects that people enjoy and can use," he said. "I'm as happy doing this as anything I've ever done in my life. I'm as busy as I've ever been, and I expect I'll keep busy until I physically can't do it anymore.

"You know, my corporate career provided enormous satisfaction in the beginning. But the higher up the ladder I went, the less I was involved with the creative process, and the less satisfying it became. I don't think I experienced a whole lot of joy in the later part of my career," he concluded.

"Today, I don't miss 'working' at all. In fact, I feel totally liberated. I have more solitude than I've had in many years, but I'm comfortable with the solitude. I feel very blessed."

"What's the downside to all this?" I asked.

"There is no downside," he replied. "I need to earn money at this, so I'm conscious of that. I want to push the envelope and make serious money. But I don't see any downside. On the contrary, I feel nothing but a powerful sense of optimism and joy."

I asked him for his advice for others regarding their retirement.

"Find a passion, something you really love to do," he responded. "I can't imagine what retirement would be without it."

"But how do you go about finding one," I asked. "So many people don't know where to start."

Richard thought for a moment. "You have to be open to trying lots of different things. Take classes. Read magazines. Talk to people. Go to shows. The more open you are, the greater the chances that you'll find something that gets you excited. Then just go for it! See how far you can take it. That's my plan. I expect to follow this new path I'm on for as long as I'm able. I've had one thirty-year career. I figure, why not another?"

THE NEW MEXICO DREAMCATCHER PROJECT

If you've ever driven through New Mexico, you've seen the vast desert spread out before you, mile after mile. It still feels like pioneer country, small towns so few and far between. Betty and Jim Claypool had driven up to Socorro from their town of Bent (population 400) in the southern part of New Mexico; I'd come in from Albuquerque, up north. We met at Martha's Black Dog Café to talk about Betty's dreamcatchers.

"This project began because of our gratitude to the Shriners," Betty said. "For years, our young son, Jack, had had difficulty walking. We took him to twenty-one doctors and no one knew what was wrong. His legs became crooked and he could no longer walk. Then we heard that the Shriners helped crippled children. We took him to their hospital in Los Angeles and within minutes of seeing him, they diagnosed his condition— juvenile rheumatoid arthritis. Finally, we knew what we were dealing with, and we could treat and try to prevent Jack from becoming permanently disabled. We were so grateful."

Twenty-five years later in 1996, the Claypools were in Galveston on vacation and learned of the Shriners Burn Institute for Children located there. Remembering how the Shriners had helped their son so many years before, they decided to stop by to say thank you. The hospital administrator was impressed with their story, and took them on a tour of the thirty-bed Burn Institute where children from all over the world are treated. He told them that one of the most difficult things about treating burn victims is that they relive their trauma in nightmares. Betty commented, "In New Mexico, we have something to fix that—dreamcatchers. I'll send dreamcatchers for your children to help them through their nightmares."

Impressed with Betty's sincerity, the hospital administrator challenged her: "A lot of people make promises when visiting here, but few follow through."

"I didn't forget my promise; I couldn't," Betty said. "Back home in Bent a few months later, Jim and I became active with the fire department, teaching school children how to prevent burns. In the process, I met the art teacher at Mescalero Apache Elementary School and the sponsor of the Indian Club at the Tularosa Middle School. I asked them if their school children could make dreamcatchers for the burned children at the Shriners Hospital. They both jumped at the opportunity to have their students do something to help others, especially using aspects of their native culture."

Expanding the project was not difficult. Twenty-two volunteer fire departments serve the small communities of their county. Betty and Jim met with each one, showed the videotape the Shriners had sent describing their work and the need to help these burned children, and asked for their support. All twenty-two Otero County Volunteer Fire Departments voted unanimously to sponsor the dreamcatcher project. Schools, and then other groups that heard of the project, began making dreamcatchers for the burned children. They were sent on to Galveston as they were made.

"Then 9/11 happened," Betty continued. "Television announcers kept showing firefighters sitting with their heads in their hands, talking about how ground zero images were burned into their brains—still there, even when they closed their eyes at night. I wanted to help. How could we send dreamcatchers to New York?

"On Thursday morning, September 13th, I called the governor's office and ended up speaking to the lieutenant governor's chief of staff. I told him my idea of making the dreamcatcher project a state-wide effort for the New York firefighters. He didn't hesitate."

"Start now!" he said.

"Then I called our local firefighters to get their support and our deputy fire chief asked, "Is it doable?" I lay awake all night pondering that question. How could we get children in all of New Mexico's schools making dreamcatchers? How would we collect them, and get them to New York? Who would we give them to once we got them there? Towards dawn, I came up with what I thought would be a workable plan. It occurred to me that banks throughout the state might be good collection points. Every little town has a bank. Yes?

"That day I called the state Fire Fighters Association, the state Superintendent of Schools, the state Fire Marshall, the New Mexico Agency for Aging, and the Banking Institution of New Mexico. Everyone gave their blessings to the project and Wells Fargo Banks agreed to be our official collection points throughout the state."

A web master and Betty collaborated to establish a website for the New Mexico Dreamcatcher Project, providing statewide, easy access to online information and instructions for making dreamcatchers. Newspapers and television advertised the project. Soon school children, senior citizens, Boy and Girl Scout troops, and other groups became involved. Betty enlisted donations of feathers and various materials for making the dreamcatchers from around the state, and had them sent to the schools and senior centers. Seniors were in the schools, teaching the children. Betty's husband was working right along with her, eighteen hours a day. The project was up and running.

Each finished dreamcatcher was slipped into a plastic baggie with a dreamcatcher notecard attached, telling the story—that the webbing was there to catch the bad dreams and have them burned off in the morning sun, the hole in the center allowing the good dreams to pass through and be fulfilled in the dreamer's destiny. Each card was signed by the person making it, along with any personal message they wished to include. "It was touching to see the children clutching their dreamcatchers to their chests as they prayed over them before they sent them on. The seniors did the same."

In two months, the people in the large and small scattered communities of New Mexico made ten thousand dreamcatchers! On November 26, 2001, in a ceremony held in the State Capitol Rotunda in Sante Fe, six Native American medicine men and women blessed the ten thousand dreamcatchers on display and the delegation present. Mail Boxes, Etc. personnel graciously packed all the dreamcatchers in bubblewrap and shipped them to New York at the company's expense. They were sent to New York's deputy fire inspector who, ironically, had once been the first fire chief of the Otero County Volunteer Firefighter's Association when he'd lived in Alamogordo years before.

Led by New Mexico's lieutenant governor and Betty, the delegation presented the dreamcatchers to the New York Fire Department on November 29, and met with Mayor Guiliani's staff at City Hall. A Mescalero Apache medicine man and the lieutenant governor appeared with Bryant Gumbel on the *Early Morning Show*, presenting him with a dreamcatcher. With Governor Patake's blessings, their group toured the horrific ruins caused by the 9/11 attack.

"I'll never forget two New York City policemen at ground zero," Betty said. "I asked if they would like a dreamcatcher and each said yes. I told them the dreamcatcher story. As I gave them their dreamcatchers and hugged first one, then the other, I could feel their chests through their bulletproof vests, heaving from the sobs they tried to stifle. It broke my heart. I wanted to take away their pain but I could not."

The letter of commendation Betty and Jim later received from the lieutenant governor began with "Well, you did it!" Today, dreamcatchers continue to be donated to the Shriners Burn Institute in Galveston, Texas, and now to the children's hospitals in New Mexico. Betty's dream is that someday schools and senior centers around the state will independently take on the support of a hospital or a group in need.

"Your original plan was to provide something of comfort to hospitalized children," I said. "I'm sure people everywhere could do something similar—not dreamcatchers, perhaps—but some sort of craft project—teddy bears, dolls, blankets—for sick and at-risk children. How would you recommend they get started?"

"First, call Public Relations at the hospital or facility you have in mind to see if they'll accept your gifts. Find out how many they can use, and how often. Then you need a platform. I got that through the Otero Volunteer Fire Department. They were our support system and our platform. You need a name that will provide legitimacy to your project and that will back you. Next, you need a plan. Who's going to do all of this? Will it be seniors working with children? We learned what an incredible resource our seniors and children in New Mexico are. You've got to totally believe in what you're doing to be able to sustain your enthusiasm. And last, but probably most important, your project must be doable.

"Retirement is a wonderful thing," Betty continued. "It gives you the time to pursue the things that are important to you. Imagine trying to do the Dreamcatcher Project if we were still employed. Jim and I have been married for forty-four years. We're best friends, so its easy being retired together and working on projects close to our hearts.

"What would you recommend to others about to retire?" I asked.

"Get a passion," Betty responded, without hesitation. "Ask yourself, 'what am I interested in'? Go take a class. Get involved in something you haven't had time to do. Get out. Don't be self-absorbed. So many people look inward instead of outward. Look at your neighborhood. Look at your larger neighborhood. Don't be afraid. Just step out."

Well-spoken from a woman who, at age sixty-three, organized her entire state.

RURAL HERITAGE
AT ITS BEST

The farmers of Washington County, Maryland, had dreamed of preserving their history, maybe in some sort of agricultural exposition. Five years ago when they decided to put their dreams into action, they asked Merwin Hans to join them. Merwin had moved to Boonesboro in his early sixties after he'd retired from the Department of Labor in Washington, D.C. He'd become active in local affairs, serving on various community boards. "I had a different set of skills to bring to the team," Merwin said. "I didn't know farming or the history of the community, and I didn't have any wonderful artifacts packed away in the attic. But I'd spent years managing large scale programs, writing, computing, working with grant money, and budgeting. And those skills proved helpful to our work."

The University of Maryland Agricultural Research Center resides on six hundred acres in Washington County. University officials gave fifty-five acres to the county to establish a park dedicated to rural education. The state agreed to give $350,000 to construct a building at the park, providing the community would match that amount. "Farmers don't sit around on their behinds waiting for people to do things," Merwin said. Without a single bake sale or car wash, the farmers raised $350,000 in donations. They were off and running. They had decided to build a museum!

"We held monthly meetings, wrote our bylaws and a museum handbook, and named our venture the Rural Heritage Museum. We decided to collect only things in use prior to 1940." Out of the attics and barns of Washington County came an amazing assortment of implements, vehicles, equipment, furniture, kitchenware, hardware, and dry goods. "A Conestoga wagon, valued at seventy-five thousand dollars, was loaned to our collection. That courting buggy over there is in perfect condition," Merwin said, pointing to the buggy with the turquoise-fringed umbrella top. The collection assembled was enough for a large display of vehicles, farm equipment and implements, and to furnish a country store, a blacksmith's shop, a post office, a typical bedroom and sitting room, and a church.

They built a seventy-two hundred square foot museum. For $500, they purchased professional museum software and began the task of sorting, labeling and documenting each donation's date of arrival, donor, and description. Members of the team went to Michigan to learn from the people at the Dearborn Museum. "You've got to tell a story so that visiting the museum will be an educational experience. Otherwise, we're just assembling a bunch of junk," Merwin said. "Joining the American Association of State and Local Museums and the Oral History Association has been helpful."

Merwin felt that visitors needed an orientation before they went into the museum itself. So with a videographer, a professional narrator and $5,000 in funds, he produced a seventeen-minute orientation video that compares life on a farm today with life prior to 1940.

In May 2001, the museum opened to the public. Its a first-class operation, staffed by volunteers. "At Christmas, we had an open house with Christmas trees, cookies, punch and Santa.

We were open six hours and over six hundred people signed our guest book," Merwin said, smiling. "The community has really embraced this place."

Now Merwin and teachers in the county are working on a video for third graders. One hundred copies will go into the schools. The narrators of the film will be children: two dressed in period clothing, two in today's wear. They'll compare life in Washington County prior to 1940 and today. Teachers will show the film in their classrooms before the children's field trips to the museum.

"I'm also working on a museum brochure. We're going to print forty thousand copies. This summer there will be another reenactment of the Battle of Antietam. Sixteen thousand men will assemble just down the road at the battlefield to reenact the Civil War's bloodiest day in which twenty-three thousand men lost their lives. We'll be putting our brochure in each one of the packets that are mailed to the reenactors prior to the event. We expect the influx of tourists to bring us hundreds of visitors.

"One of my main functions has been to collect money for all the things we need. So we formed a 501(c)3 organization, Friends of the Washington County Rural Heritage Museum. Members pay dues—some give a little, some give a lot—and that's how we fund the project. Once we've been in business for three years, we can go to the state of Maryland for grants."

Merwin's advice to others who might want to preserve their history is as follows:

1. Find others who want to join you. Who are the preservationists? Connect with the historical society. Gather kindred spirits.
2. Determine what you want to do—your mission and goals.
3. Who might be your source of funding? Is there a piece of property or an old building you could renovate and use?
4. Plan, plan, plan. Do it right. Make it a quality endeavor.
5. Don't get too expansive. Let it grow naturally. If there's community support, it will happen.

Merwin is now eighty-one. "If I have any regrets about retirement, and I don't have many, its that I didn't get started with something meaningful earlier. I worked in my garden and on the farm, and got a real estate license. I spent several years buying, refurbishing, and selling houses. But I like giving back. Not stuffing envelopes, mind you. I like using my skills. I've enjoyed being active because I like to work; I respect work. And you need work and being with other people to be stimulated.

"We have more work ahead of us at the museum. Someday, we'd like to have a paid staff member. We're constructing another building for tractors, manure spreaders, and all the large farm equipment. And we have plans for a Heritage Village—one that will include barns, a windmill, farm house, pig house and shed.

"It's been a labor of love for the people who have lived on this land for generation after generation. I've enjoyed being a part of it."

SWEETPEA AND
BUTTERCUP

The children giggled and squealed. Water squirted from the flower on Buttercup's lapel, and as he shook hands with each of Mrs. Collier's second graders, his hand would squeak and his elbow "honked." Could there be anything more glorious for a seven-year-old than having his grandparents, Sweetpea and Buttercup, visit his class?

Sue and Mike Turk of Short Hills, New Jersey—*aka* Sweetpea and Buttercup—are therapeutic clowns. Years ago, when their children were young and Sue was still employed as a speech and language pathologist, she got involved in clowning through the Pioneers, AT&T's service organization. When Mike, an AT&T executive, later retired, they began clowning together at children's birthday parties, schools, and hospitals. It was fun, but didn't quite bring the satisfaction they were after.

Mike was on the board at their synagogue, and one day he and the rabbi got into quite a discussion about clowning. Mike told the rabbi he and Sue wanted clowning to be more than bringing smiles. They wanted to use clowning as a means to entertain and communicate with those in need—maybe the sick and the elderly—and in so doing, provide a more meaningful experience for themselves and others who might take up clowning. As the discussion continued, the rabbi mentioned the need for a service project in which the youth of the congregation could be involved. *Voila!* Clowning and young people—a perfect match! Mitzvah Clowns was born.

"Mitzvah is Hebrew and means our obligation to do good for others," said Mike. "Clowning would be a way for the youth of the congregation to learn about mitzvah by doing. We designed a day-long program which would include a morning class that would first focus on learning about mitzvah and biblical references to doing good, and then move on to clowning—applying make-up, dressing in costume, ballooning, and how to interact with the audience (unlike the clowns we might see in the circus, therapeutic clowns speak.) After lunch, we'd transport the new clowns to nursing homes, assisted-living residences and hospitals where they could apply what they'd learned."

"It really seemed to work," Sue said. "We had ten adolescents and adults in our first class. They loved it, and the patients did, too. Clowning is just a vehicle to get sick and elderly people to smile, open up, and for a short time be distracted from their illness or other problems. And there's something especially endearing about young people as clowns. Mike and I were delighted with how it worked out. We found teaching others—a kind of passing of the torch—immensely satisfying. This is what we'd been looking for."

From that time on, Congregation B'nai Israel signed on as the official sponsor of Mitzvah Clowns, and participating in mitzvah clowning became a part of being bar or bat mitzvah at B'nai Israel and many other nearby synagogues. Sweetpea and Buttercup (they train in costume) have now trained over eight hundred kids and adults. They teach at religious schools, middle schools, high schools and colleges.

"When a child who hasn't spoken for over a week smiles and says 'Hi', that's important," said Sue. "Once an older woman in a nursing home who was in a wheelchair, asked Buttercup if he'd dance with her. She was sobbing. She hadn't danced in several years. You know that dance was important to her, and to us. Doctors tell us recovery time can be reduced by happiness. Everybody wins, and it's therapeutic for us, as well."

None of this comes without cost. Sue and Mike charge each student $35 (their cost) for a kit consisting of make-up, mirrors, brushes, and a guide to mitzvah clowning. In the past, financial aid came from a one-year grant from the New Jersey Healthcare Foundation. More recently, Sue and Mike have received honorariums to help defray the expenses of costumes and wigs which they supply for the training session, and for other materials, printing costs, transportation and overnight travel expenses, should that be necessary. They continue to pursue funding from grants to cover their growing expenses. "Our goal," said Mike, "is to spread Mitzvah Clowns everywhere, as far and as wide as it can go. That's why we like to work with kids. We hope that some of them will latch on to the idea and continue to clown as adults. I'm happy to say some already have.

"During the past year, we've held weekend seminars in Rhode Island, New York, Texas, North Carolina and Florida. We've produced two videos: a three-minute public relations (PR) video and a ten-minute preview of our classes and excerpts from our performances. And we have our own website. These weekend seminars now include training new Mitzvah Clown leaders, as well as clowns. During this past year, we were part of a TV documentary on Jewish education which was aired on ABC."

Nowadays, Sue and Mike have so many commitments it's a bit overwhelming. "We have classes scheduled for the next six weekends," said Sue. "Our preference would be a maximum of two classes a month. Any day we're teaching is a long, ten-hour day. We put on our costumes and make-up before we leave home or our motel room, drive to the class location, teach the class, go to the nursing home or hospital, drive back to the classroom site with the group, then back home, and remove our makeup." For thirty years, Sue has been a diabetic and is currently on an insulin pump. She's also on the list for a kidney transplant. She is careful to avoid insulin reactions during the course of these long training days.

"We're at a crossroads," she continued. "Mitzvah Clowns has become so big that we've added an administrator to take care of scheduling and other administrative matters. We're gradually turning over some of the training to others, but this is our baby. It's sometimes hard to relinquish control."

Now in their mid-sixties, Sue and Mike are trying to figure out what's next. One project on the front burner is a New Jersey Mitzvah Clown Consortium. "We're very happy with what we're doing. We'll never stop clowning. There's so much satisfaction and we've had a positive impact on so many lives. It's just a question of how much energy we'll be able to devote to this as we get older."

How does one go about getting into clowning?

"Many community centers offer clowning classes," Mike said. "Or, come to New Jersey, or, better yet, invite us to teach in your community! You can find good material for costumes at Good Will, the Salvation Army or in your own attic. Wigs and make-up are usually available at costume or novelty stores."

I asked Sue and Mike their thoughts about retirement.

Mike said, "I think some of us have difficulty. I, for one, didn't know what to do with myself at first. I helped a couple of friends run their businesses for the first three years, but I'd recommend people start thinking about what they want to do before they retire, not after. I think a lot of us can't even visualize all the wonderful possibilities. None of us wants to retire to a void. The trick is to stay open to the opportunities that are out there."

Sue continued. "I've always wanted to know about life and about people. I'm always asking about things. You can find out all sorts of interesting things to do just by talking with people. Our friends and relatives are often doing neat things, or they know others who are. Take advantage of organizations like the

Y, churches, synagogues. Everything is connected to everything. You never know what will lead to new opportunities and new friends."

"That's another thing I've discovered," Mike said. "Your friends, and the need for friends, is even greater when you retire. You're in a new ball game. It can be hard to continue those work relationships once you've left the workplace. I think friendship is a big issue in retirement. One good friend can make all the difference."

Sweetpea and Buttercup have made many friends through clowning. "There's a magic to clowning," said Mike. "You get a chance to jump out of yourself." And teaching others about that magic has given Sue and Mike the kind of enjoyment, meaning and substance they wanted their retirement to be about.

SOUP'S ON!

"I don't know what possessed me," said Arnold Siegel, seventy, of Santa Clara, California. "It's not like I'd been dying to be a chef all my life. But a few years before I retired from Lockheed, while visiting my mother in a convalescent home in San Francisco, I walked into their kitchen and proclaimed, 'What a wonderful place to cook!' The startled kitchen staff urged me to join them, and that's how it started. I was their only volunteer, and I've been a volunteer chef ever since.

"The head cook taught me everything I know. I'd drive one hundred miles round trip on Saturday—sometimes, Sundays and holidays—and we'd fix two entrees, and three vegetables for dinner—elegant fare. This place was something: waiters in black tie, white, starched table linens, fresh flowers on every table. Plush, everyday. By the end of the year, I was doing it all—salmon, prime rib. Money was no object. The 150 residents would get all dressed up for dinner. These little old ladies loved dinnertime. My engineering career had never been this satisfying," Arnold exclaimed.

"I retired in 1992 and continued volunteering there for a couple more years. Then one day, while I was out bicycling, I saw the Sunnyvale Nutrition Center. It's actually a senior center. I walked in and asked, 'Need a cook?' The rest, as they say, is history. The senior center was so much closer to home than the convalescent home, so I switched. For six years, five days a week, I cooked at Sunnyvale. We provided lunch every day for $1.70.

"Then I learned that Our Daily Bread, the soup kitchen at St. Thomas Episcopal Church in Sunnyvale, needed a Wednesday cook. I thought it might be a nice change of pace working there one day a week, while still cooking the other four days at the senior center. Four years later, the head cook at Our Daily Bread announced that he was having physical problems, and would need someone to take over the operation as he convalesced.

"I'd never been a boss. Never wanted to be a boss before. But I thought, 'Here's my chance to see how it feels. I'll do this for three months while Joe's gone.' I was nervous at first, made a few mistakes, got help, and eventually got it. Joe didn't come back, as it turned out, so I've been the head cook since January 2002. Before, I worked five days a week and it was really too much. Here we operate Monday, Wednesday and Friday, which is much better for me.

"You have to be creative in this job. We get most of our food from a food bank and from donations, and we never know what they'll have available for us. We don't have the luxury of purchasing whatever we'd like as we did at the convalescent home and the senior center. Here we create our menus mostly from whatever is donated.

"I like making decisions. I'm proud of being head cook. It means a lot more responsibility. We provide both a regular meal and a vegetarian meal for our diners, and peanut butter and jelly sandwiches for the children. Sometimes I come in on Tuesdays and Thursdays to prepare. I love doing the prep work—cutting, slicing, dicing—and when you're cooking for between two hundred fifty and three hundred people there can be a lot of it. We get turkeys sometimes, and have to bake them a day in advance or we'd never be ready for lunch at eleven fifteen. This morning I came in at six thirty because today's menu required extra time. When eleven comes, the doors open and the diners have the next fifteen minutes to get their drinks and settle in their seats. We have to be ready to serve at eleven fifteen.

"Two days a week, I have one helper; on Fridays I have two. We serve leftovers (seconds) from the previous meal after twelve noon, and many people stay for both meals. We have servers and cleanup staff as well, and all of us are volunteers. It's a very loving atmosphere in which to work. We have fun, and we all want to give. Before each meal, we form a circle, join hands, and have prayer time. That means a lot to me.

"A lot of the people we serve are homeless. Many come with their children, some come in cars, on buses, some walk. We never turn anyone away or "qualify" them in any way. I love seeing the people eating, hearing their compliments. I'm a very private person and enjoy my alone time, but here we're friends and I have my social time."

How do you orchestrate a soup kitchen? Arnold offers these pointers:

1. It works best when it's all-volunteer. Competition often enters into it when there are both paid staff and volunteers.
2. There should be one person in charge of menus who makes sure the cook has all the ingredients and equipment that will be needed.
3. You'll need a good recipe book. Our recipes all serve 250 people.
4. Make sure you have a good staff of cooks, clean-up folks, servers and prep people.
5. If you make arrangements with your local supermarket, they'll give you a lot of baked goods. They get tax write-offs for their donations.

6. We serve our meals; people do not have to stand in line. We try to be very fast and have all our guests graciously served in fifteen minutes.
7. Be clear about what time your guests should come, and when they should go. Ask them to be respectful of the dining room rules. Our guests get their own drinks, sit where they like, and wait to be served.

"I love retirement," Arnold said. "I had the most interesting job at Lockheed—secret, secret, very unique—but the politics drove me crazy. Now, each meal we prepare is an enjoyable project, I have good friends, and there's no red tape or politics. I don't want anyone to tell me what to do anymore. I've done all that."

Arnold's suggestions for those about to retire are as follows:

1. Make a list of all the things you'd like to do.
2. Then make sure you have the money you'll need to do them. Forget about worrisome, aggressive investments.
3. Make sure you stay active and get out of the house and get into some sort of project. I'm an avid biker. I have a computer but haven't gone online because I'm afraid I'd end up spending hours on it.
4. Help others.
5. Think ahead about how you're going to stay active. I found something I love. I have some friends from Lockheed who hated retirement because they weren't doing anything, and they went back to work!

"I could never go back to working for money again. Fortunately, I have enough income to take care of myself. I've carved out a new life, and I love life in the kitchen with the other volunteers. It's home."

A KENTUCKY
CRAFTSMAN

In the picturesque town of Danville, Kentucky, sits Charles Hamblin's house, right there on Main Street. Not a shed, or barn, or basement or garage. A whole house devoted to his woodworking.

Before he retired from American Greetings, Charles had bought the house to fix up and sell. He'd done that previously and made a good profit. But the more he thought about it, the more he thought it would be a great woodworking shop. Charles' wife, Josephine, was always asking him to do this project or that. Over the years he'd accumulated band saws, lathes, and other woodworking equipment, and he needed a larger place in which to work. So he moved all his equipment to the house on Main Street.

"It looks like a haunted house," Charles cautioned, as we walked in. "It wasn't in real good shape when I bought it, and I haven't made it look any better." The old, yellowed shades are drawn, and every room contains machinery and wood—piles of lumber here and there, crown molding that Charles got at an auction, a stack of dowels he bought when a business went bankrupt.

"I didn't retire until I was seventy-one because I was afraid I'd be bored. I spent the first year working on things for the house. I loved being here in my shop, but wasn't sure what I'd do when I got caught up on all the projects. Then my daughter gave me a book on bird carving. I used to whittle in my youth, and thought bird carving might be fun. So I tried. My first bird was a wren, because it's small and I know how wrens look.

"The book diagrammed what to do. You cut a block of wood down to the size you'll want, and draw a silhouette of the bird on opposite sides of the block. You use the band saw to cut out the rough shape, and then you start carving. This is where patience comes in. You can't go fast. You carve out a little piece at a time.

"When you get your shape the way you want it, you start drawing the feathers," he continued. Each feather is gone over with a wood burner, strand after strand. Once the bird has been textured, Charles coats it with shellac, and then begins patiently applying the acrylic washes. Layer by layer, he builds the color and patterns of the birds.

"It takes me about a month to do a large bird—maybe a week for a small one. Naturally, my results weren't that good when I started. But you learn by doing. You do it mostly by eye. You look over your work, look at your mistakes, and see how you can improve."

Charles has read all kinds of books, and he's gone to many woodworking shows, and still does. "You can learn a lot just watching the carving demonstrations and attending the seminars. And everything you'd ever need for carving can be purchased at the shows—glass eyes and the pewter feet for your birds; blocks of specialty woods. "The National Wood Carvers Association has a good magazine called *Chip Chats*. It lists all the shows to be offered in the U.S. during the year—well over one hundred of them. And there's one show devoted entirely to bird carving that is held in Iowa each year. It's great. You get humble real fast when you go to those shows."

Now seventy-six, Charles says he has a great life. "I love the relaxation of doing this; the fun of taking nothing and making something out of it. There's no rush. Painting may take a week or a little more. And then you build a stand or perch for the bird, and try to be a little creative with it. The days go so fast."

On any given day Charles spends the mornings at his woodworking house. He goes home for lunch and spends the afternoon with Josephine. After a five o'clock supper, Charles heads back to his shop until nine.

Advice Charles would give to others wanting to learn a craft? "Don't give up too quickly. For awhile, what you're working on doesn't look like what you intended, but just keep working at it. Go watch someone else do it. Go to the shows. Take classes. Read books. Look on the Internet. Join the association for your craft—there will be one."

Charles says local clubs centered around your general interests can also be helpful. "Here in Danville, we have a group called 'The Gathering Artists.' We meet once a month and share our work, discuss upcoming local arts and crafts activities, and let everyone know where our work will be displayed that month. It's fun. Our work is solitary, so we enjoy this community."

After only three years of bird carving, Charles regularly displays his birds at local businesses and at the library. Recently, the Gallery on the Square in Danville had a showing of the works of forty Kentucky artists. Twelve of Charles' birds were displayed and on sale for several hundred dollars each. "I enjoy sharing my work with others. I don't have financial ambitions, but it's a good way to meet people."

Charles says everyone should find something they like to do. "If I'd known I was going to get into bird carving, I wouldn't have dreaded retirement. I think people need to find whatever it is they want to do *before* they retire. Then they'll be looking forward to it."

"I guess most of my life has been like the bumble bee's. Aerodynamically, the bumble bee shouldn't be able to fly. His body is too big and thick, his wings are too short. But the bumble bee doesn't know he can't fly, so he goes ahead and flies anyway.

"Everyone should try flying," Charles said, smiling.

ON THE WAY
TO GENEALOGY

Beverley Lee Cole Cullen didn't intend to be an activist. Her passion for genealogy has been her focus since she retired from her job as a management analyst at the IRS in the 1980s. Since then, she's conducted years of investigation and plans to write a book about it as soon as her research is complete. But other things have kept popping up, and Beverley has taken a few detours.

Shortly after she retired, Beverley's neighborhood of eighteen hundred homes in Loudoun County, Virginia, experienced a crime wave. Her home was burglarized, and like other concerned homeowners, she attended a community meeting. It was clear the homeowners needed someone to develop a strategy for the group. "I spent the next three months working full-time designing a plan for us, and that got us started. I recruited and trained eighty-nine block captains, and we were able to obtain a registry of homeowners' cars and license plate numbers so those not from the neighborhood would be easy to spot."

Homeowners were shown how to install security devices on their windows and doors. "Operation Identification" was initiated to provide a system for marking objects of value in the home, so they'd be difficult to sell if stolen. Neighbors were urged to look out for one another. Beverley led the effort through bi-monthly block captain meetings. "Our plan had the full support of the sheriff's department," she said, "and eighteen months after we began, the crime rate had been reduced by 50 percent."

Beverley decided it was time for her to travel and get back to genealogy, so she turned over the leadership of the neighborhood watch effort to someone else. Off she went on tours of Scandinavia, China, Africa, New Zealand, Australia, Mexico and Canada. In between, she worked on her family history.

"But during the 1990s, growth and traffic around here had mushroomed out of control," Beverley said. "Subdivisions were going up, and developers were bearing no responsibility for the county infrastructure necessary to support their developments. Real estate property taxes were soaring. Loudoun was the third fastest growing county in the U.S.

"I began attending meetings of the County Board of Supervisors and public hearings. I spoke out on the effect the growth and subsequent tax increases were having on seniors. Many who had been residents for decades were forced to sell their homes and leave." Beverley discovered that seniors were entitled to real estate tax reductions, providing their gross income was no higher than $40,000 and net worth no greater than $150,000, excluding the value of their home. The trouble was, there had been no cost of living adjustments to the program in the past seven years, and Beverley wanted that addressed.

"I wrote to the chairman and every member of the board of supervisors, calling their attention to this matter. Then I learned that the county couldn't change its income caps unless the enabling legislation was first passed by the state. So I changed my focus and began lobbying the state legislature."

Beverley called and wrote to her state senator and delegate. She provided them with statistics showing the increases in the cost of living and consumer price index over the past seven years. The legislators quickly agreed the income caps were out of date. When the legislature next met, they introduced a bill changing the income levels for seniors to reflect current cost of living. In 1998, the bill passed with no difficulty.

Then Beverley went back to work in the county. She drew up a petition, collected signatures, and spoke to senior clubs and church groups to inform them of the need to update this legislation. She urged them to call their supervisors. She wrote letters to the editor, committee chairpersons, and county supervisors. Once again, she voiced her concerns at the supervisors' meetings until the county cap was finally changed.

Now Loudoun County's income cap for the tax reduction program has been raised twice in the last three years— the gross income cap is now $62,000, the net worth cap $240,000. And for the first time, this benefit for seniors is being widely publicized in local newspapers and county publications. Many more seniors are now able to qualify for the tax reduction and remain residents of the county.

Beverley resumed her work on genealogy. But the community center, playground, and the eighteen-mile walking trail in her neighborhood needed serious attention. Under the existing financial structure of the homeowners association, there was no way to pay for these improvements.

"I knew that getting the homeowners association designated as a 501(c)4 organization could reduce our taxes, thus making more funds available for improvements. In addition, if we formed a 501(c)3 organization to support the homeowners association, that would give us a mechanism for soliciting donations. It took over a year, but after many setbacks, and months of phone calls and letters, the IRS finally approved both these designations. Now the community has money from two new sources."

In a world where its purported that one person can no longer make a difference, Beverley's a great example to the contrary.

She's tenacious. When she sees something that needs to be fixed, she goes after it and stays with it until it's been made right.

"Well, I believe we have no right to complain unless we're willing to do something about it. That's just how I was raised," Beverley said.

What advice would Beverley give to others working in their communities? She offers seven suggestions:

1. Attend community meetings so that you are familiar with what's happening—newspaper accounts may not be current or complete.
2. Learn the details of the situation.
3. Enlist support from others—attend meetings as a group.
4. Find out whom you need to contact and influence to gain support.
5. Dig for the information you need to make your case. Back it up with facts and history.
6. If your issue is important to many constituents, raise it in an election year. Politicians are usually more responsive then.
7. Communicate pleasantly, but firmly.

Beverley loves retirement and encourages everyone to get involved in their community. "It's amazing how much we can accomplish by refusing to sit on the sidelines. I've always had a lot of irons in the fire," she added. "Retirement gives me the time to pursue them. The more interested I am in things and the more I care, the more fun I have. And computers make it even more exciting, because they open so many doors.

"I would tell others to jump into retirement with all four feet! It's such a wonderful time. Get thoroughly engrossed in whatever interests you. And take good care of your health so you'll have the energy and vitality to pursue it."

Now, at age seventy-six, Beverley says it is truly, absolutely, positively, time for her to get back to genealogy.

THE ANSWER
TO A PRAYER

T o listen to Don Reeves tell it at the National Cowboy & Western Heritage Museum in Oklahoma City, Dr. Autry Brown was the answer to his prayer. The museum had moved to its beautiful new facility, lots of changes were taking place, and on their doorstep arrived four palettes of barbed wire. "Barbed wire?" I asked, puzzled. "Why would you purchase barbed wire?"

"Well, the invention of barbed wire had as much influence on the settlement of the American West as the revolver and the repeating rifle," Don replied. "Because of that, the museum selected more than eight thousand pieces of barbed wire for purchase. But now we had to sort it, identify it, tag it, and figure out how to display it. And then out of the blue, I met Dr. Autry Brown of Bolivar, Missouri."

Autry had begun collecting barbed wire in 1968. He was a Baptist minister back then and was looking for an inexpensive hobby that he and his young son could share. A friend gave him four pieces of barbed wire to get them started. "It was a good hobby, involving lots of history and stories," Autry said.

"We'd spend Saturday mornings out in the country, looking for abandoned, 'downed' fences. We enjoyed walking in the fields and picking up pieces of wire. Ranchers appreciate you getting those pieces so their cows don't step on them.

"From Illinois west, there are a lot of collectors of wire, and they swap and sell at wire shows. We were living in Colorado at the time and joined the Colorado Wire Collectors Association. We went to wire shows, and over time we built up quite a collection.

"My son grew up, we moved to Missouri, and I put a hold on collecting for quite a while. Then one day after I retired, my wife, Irene, and I were going to a Barbed Wire Show and stopped in Oklahoma City to visit what was then called the Cowboy Hall of Fame. The museum had twenty pieces of shorty wire (four and one half inches long) displayed.

"A man who looked important was standing close by and I asked, 'Are you connected with the museum?' The man was Don Reeves, McCasland Chair of Cowboy Culture at the museum. I told him, 'This display has an erroneous implication in it. It's based on out-of-date information. I'm not trying to criticize. I'm a collector.' Don was keenly interested in what I had to say and took us out back to show us the palettes of barbed wire they'd just received, and told us about the monumental task before them.

"Irene and I talked it over and a few weeks later I called Don and told him I might be interested in helping them identify their wire. Don was delighted. From then on, Irene and I would drive our recreation vehicle (RV) to Oklahoma City every month, park in the museum parking lot, and spend two weeks sorting barbed wire.

"Most collections of barbed wire are of eighteen-inch strands. Some are single strand, others double, triple and more. The barbs are all different shapes and sizes: some two points, some four, some in the shape of a star, some with pieces of wood or metal to serve as warning plates.

"Those palettes held *thirty-five thousand* pieces of barbed wire, and each one needed to be identified and classified. We sorted out the duplicates, tagged each piece, looked it up in the published books on barbed wire, numbered and priced it, and tried to find the patent. We worked on this eight hours a day, six days a week. We wrote all the information down on tablets as we were sorting so that when we went home I could enter it in the computer." By the time Autry finished at the computer, he had filled several inch-thick binders with the museum's barbed wire information.

One whole room of the sleek, new, marble Cowboy Museum is devoted to barbed wire and branding irons. There, 1,350 pieces are on display all around the room in attractive vertical drawers, 20" high by 2" wide. Each drawer contains about 20 different pieces of 18" wire "floating" between two panels of glass. A plaque on the wall of the room tells of Autry's contributions to the display.

"Irene and I thought all of this would take us about three months when we started," Autry said. "It turned out to be a year and a half. During that time, I started noticing that Irene was becoming confused. Later, she was diagnosed with Alzheimer's. Working on this project helped me get through that terrible time.

"I wanted to do this because it would help preserve a part of history," Autry continued. "In the east there were stone fences and wooden fences. But on the plains and prairie, there are neither stones nor trees, so ranchers used barbed wire instead. Fences were used to keep the cattle in, or out."

In 2001, Autry contacted Don again. "I've been thinking we need pictures of all that wire. We can put the pictures on a CD, and eventually put them in a book. Both the Cowboy Museum and I could benefit from this endeavor. There are a lot of mistakes in books out there. I would like to update them with the new information that is now readily available."

Don was enthusiastic about Autry's idea. Using a digital camera, six flood lights and a light stand, Autry photographs four wires at a time, and then cuts and pastes so that four individual pictures are the result. Eventually, he expects to have a book displaying two thousand strands, with accompanying information.

"Do you think other hobbyists around the country could contribute to museums as you've done, Autry?" I asked.

"Absolutely. If you have a hobby that has historical value, contact a museum. Every hobby is on the Internet, has shows and swap meets, and its own magazines. All of those outlets can point hobbyists to the museums.

"If people don't have hobbies, but would like to become collectors, all they need to do is go to shows featuring antiques and collectibles to get ideas for themselves. Out here there are antique collector shows with displays of cattle brands, antique nails, door knobs, milk bottles, you name it. You can usually get a feel for the hobby by talking to the vendors, and they can tell you of upcoming shows and give you literature. Just remember to ask yourself how much your new hobby is going to cost you, and whether you've got a place to put it.

"I have so many things I want to do in retirement," Autry continued. "Someday I want to write my memoirs for my children and grandchildren. I don't understand people who retire and do nothing. When are they going to blow away and die? I'd rather wear out than rust out, but who says we have to do either?

"Irene was in a nursing home for five years. When I committed her to the home, I cried, slept, and prayed for three days. Barbed wire kept me busy and my mind occupied. I visited her every day and tried to be there at the same time, hoping that regularity would be helpful to her thinking. I believe marriage is for the good times and the bad. She knew I would be there for her."

Irene died in 2001. Autry is seventy-eight now, and recently met someone new at church. "Life goes on and I'm looking forward to it," he said.

MILLIE'S HAPPY TIMES

In 1983, Millie Finkel, age fifty, of Morristown, New Jersey, was finishing chemotherapy treatment for breast cancer. It was summer and a friend asked if she'd like to be a counselor at a new camp, Camp Happy Times. Millie wasn't too keen on the idea but at her friend's urging, she agreed to go for one day only, just to see what it was like. At the end of her day at camp, Millie went home, packed her things, and returned for the rest of the week. For the next thirteen years, Millie was a counselor at this one-week camp.

Camp Happy Times is a children's oncology camp, one of seventy-five in the nation. Inner-city children with cancer— mostly black and Hispanic—come for a week's diversion from their illness. The camp is held at Tyler Hill Camp in Pennsylvania and is staffed by Tyler Hill's full compliment of coaches, instructors, life guards, kitchen and maintenance staff.

One week each year, Tyler Hill rents the camp to the Valerie Fund, a foundation that provides comprehensive health care services for children with cancer and blood disorders. The Valerie Fund recruits volunteer doctors, nurses, nurse practitioners and counselors to tend to the medical and emotional needs of the children while they're at Camp Happy Times, as well as securing the equipment and transportation that will be needed.

"I fell in love with the children during my very first visit," Millie said. "I was placed with fourteen-year-old girls. It wasn't difficult for me to identify with their bald heads, their nausea and vomiting. I felt connected to them, and when the camp was over I kept in touch."

From then on, Millie was a counselor and six years later, she was asked to be on the Board. When she became a trustee of the Valerie Fund, the fund-raising arm of Camp Happy Times, it meant attending monthly meetings, conducting fund-raisers, and speaking publicly about their cause.

"In those days, training was minimal for camp counselors," Millie said. "I could see many things that could benefit from improvement. So six years ago, I went to the Board and volunteered to be their new Director—not paid, as they'd had before, but as a volunteer." At age sixty, Millie became the full-time volunteer director of Camp Happy Times. Except for November and December during the holidays, Millie works at this job at least three to four hours every day.

Millie's duties? "Imagine taking 250 sick children away for a week. We need to put in place everything they could possibly need for this week away from home or hospital. I negotiate the contract with the camp each year, and assemble the medical team. We always have two pediatric oncologists and five pediatric oncology nurse practitioners. They come from the eight hospitals in New Jersey and New York in which the Valerie Fund has centers. We also have over one hundred volunteer counselors—one for every two children."

Every person at the camp—medical personnel, counselors and the kids themselves—must go through a rigorous application process. "A company in Montana does background checks each year on everyone connected with our camp—even me. I used to do all the interviewing, but I need to start turning some of this over to others. We are very strict about those who work with the kids—curfew strictly enforced, no drugs, alcohol, smoking, skimpy clothing, bikinis, courtships, untoward language, leaving the premises—you name it. We want a wholesome environment.

"I make sure golf carts are donated for the children who can't walk. Oxygen is generally donated and hopefully, other medical supplies as well. Each child gets a tee shirt, sweatshirt, shorts, sweat pants and a duffel bag. We have a year-long project collecting nearly-new summer clothing and sporting equipment, hats, suntan lotion, shampoo, blankets, and pillows. All of this is donated so you can imagine the work in asking for, receiving, and thanking contributors for myriad donations. And we need liability insurance for any trips we take, and buses to transport the kids to and from the camp."

A year ago, Millie chaired a conference hosted by the Valerie Fund for 250 people across the nation involved in children's oncology camps. Bernie Siegel was their keynote speaker. He spoke to them about caring for themselves as they care for others. It was a proud moment for Millie.

"I love my job. With email, a cell phone, my fax and laptop I go wherever I want—I'm not pinned down to an office. My husband and I go to Florida each winter. And if something comes up that I want to do, I feel I can change a meeting time now and then since it's a volunteer job. I wouldn't feel comfortable doing that if I were being paid.

"The best thing about my job is the children. I have a lot of young friends now. The counselors confide in me, ask me to go skiing with them—things like that. Many of them are cancer survivors like me. It keeps me young. I love using my wits and imagination daily."

When I asked Millie how one would go about getting involved, she replied, "I'd recommend they look up children's oncology camps on the Internet. Once they find one close by, they can make arrangements to go for a day. They needn't volunteer for a week as a counselor, if they'd rather not. Lots of people volunteer their services for a day. We have chefs, clowns, a stained glass instructor, therapy dogs—all come for a day. A manicurist provides manicures. A hairdresser fixes hairpieces to stick out under the children's hats. And when camp is not in session, there are always plenty of fund raising activities needing volunteers."

What does Millie think of retirement? "It's the best thing in the world!" she exclaimed. "I wish I could get my husband to retire. He's sixty-six also. But he loves his work. And I love mine. Still, we do plenty of other things. I took pottery for a few years. I'm on the Board of our Florida condominium. I go to book discussions. We go to lectures and concerts. I think you get younger in retirement, if you're busy. Pick and choose. There are so many things to do. We all have the option of learning and changing."

Millie continued. "I seem to like volunteering best. I've always been a volunteer. I learned a long time ago the importance of giving. I need to give. It makes me feel good."

WORLD EXPLORERS

For twenty years, Kathy and Rodney Kling lived and worked in Asia, Indonesia, Africa and South America. They'd gotten the bug for international travel early on when Kathy had been an exchange student to Israel during high school, and Rodney had served in China during the last days of World War II. Rodney is a teacher; Kathy, a librarian. It wasn't difficult to find work. But when Kathy's mother became ill and needed help, they interrupted their travels and went home to Durham, North Carolina.

A few years later, Kathy's mother died. Deciding to go abroad again, they thought they'd look for volunteer opportunities this time—they no longer needed to limit their search to paid employment at this point in their lives. "The Peace Corps was an obvious choice," Kathy said. "Although most volunteers are young adults, the Peace Corps welcomes senior volunteers who are in good health, particularly those with international experience.

"Their application process is extensive. They want to know about your background, interests, qualifications, and motivation. Even your doctors and dentists have to respond to application questions." Kathy went on to explain that the Peace Corps conducts a comprehensive interview. It tries to place people in locations of their choosing. She and Rodney wanted to go someplace where they'd not lived—Europe, the Caribbean, or perhaps, the South Pacific.

Then they waited. Four months later, they were notified of their assignment to Poland. Although volunteers needn't take the first offer, Kathy and Rodney were happy for the opportunity to live in Eastern Europe. A friend volunteered to oversee their property, and they rented their home, furnished. Four weeks after being notified, they reported to Washington, D.C. for three days of orientation. There they met the seventy-four other volunteers also going to Poland that year.

Once their orientation was complete, the volunteers flew to Warsaw and were taken to the small town of Radom to begin three months of language training. All seventy-six volunteers lived with non-English speaking families. "Every day, all day long, was spent in class at the technical college," Rodney said. "For the first two weeks, all of us were in the same class. Then we were separated into smaller groups according to our language abilities."

Early in the third week of training, Kathy fell and broke four bones in her foot. Although x-rays were taken in Poland, the Peace Corps promptly flew her back to Washington where she underwent surgery to have three pins inserted in her foot. Back in Poland and on crutches for the next four months, the Peace Corps paid for a taxi to take Kathy back and forth to school each day.

When language training was completed, the volunteers were officially sworn into the Peace Corps. At an impressive ceremony and party attended by all the host families, the U.S. ambassador to Poland did the honors. The volunteers received their assignments and for the first time, the group split up as each went off to the town or city that would be their new home.

Kathy and Rodney were the only volunteers sent to the town of Czechtohowa—home of the Black Madonna—and one of the most popular tourist attractions in Poland. The Black

Madonna is a painting of the Madonna housed in a local monastery. Legend has it that the painting turned black due to a miracle, and pilgrims come from all over Europe to see it, making Czechtohowa a lively place.

The Peace Corps provided Rodney and Kathy with a two-bedroom apartment in one of the block, high rise buildings built by the Russians after World War II. Outside, it was dirty and dingy, with graffiti everywhere. But inside, the apartment had ample heating and air conditioning, a tub, and a washing machine. They even had a balcony. They got BBC's *Sky News* daily on their television. By Polish standards, their apartment was plush.

The Peace Corps gave Kathy and Rodney money for food and transportation. Their employer, a private school, paid them standard Polish wages for teaching and library work. Rodney taught English to eighteen- to twenty-year-olds, while Kathy cataloged books and started an English language library.

Peace Corps volunteers work a four-day week. On their three-day weekends, the Klings went to Warsaw, Krakow and other nearby cities, or visited with Peace Corps friends. They worked a full year with time off for holidays and summer recess. With Peace Corps permission, they traveled to other countries.

When it was time for their tour to end, Kathy and Rodney informed the school's headmaster, and in Warsaw on the way home, debriefed with the Peace Corps country director.

"The Peace Corps is a first-class operation. Look at their website (www.peacecorps.gov) and you can tell," said Rodney.

"Everything is handled professionally and efficiently," Kathy added. "And we loved being around young adults and having an opportunity to mentor fellow volunteers."

Rodney said, "Their number is 1-800-424-8580. Call them. It's nice to see our government dollars being spent for such a good cause."

Now the Klings are home in Durham. Until their next international assignment, they attend classes at Duke University's Institute for Learning in Retirement, and take part in clinical trials at the medical school. "They're fun, and keep us out of trouble," Kathy said.

Kathy and Rodney never led a traditional life of structure and routine, so this time of life is not much of a change. "Retirement really doesn't apply to us," they asserted. "It's merely a term. Yet we love being able to choose what to do each day without obligation to be anywhere or do anything."

At sixty and seventy-four, respectively, Kathy and Rodney show no signs of slowing down. In a few months, they'll be interviewing to go to either Vietnam or Laos with a volunteer program out of Stanford University. "It's wonderful to spread the concept of volunteerism to other countries," Kathy said. "Volunteering is unheard of in many parts of the world. And of course, we love the adventure. We each fell in love with international travel when we were young, and we're still hooked."

AROUND THE WORLD
IN TWENTY YEARS

Dick Hunter and his wife, Mary Margaret, had talked about moving back to Colorado when he retired. And then in 1978, when Dick was sixty-four, Mary Margaret died during routine surgery.

"I had no idea what I was going to do now that Mary Margaret was gone," Dick said, "so I kept working." He'd led a typical married life until then: raising children, participating in church, and building a career with the National Mental Health Association (NMHA). He'd been there twenty-eight years.

A year after Mary Margaret's death, the World Federation for Mental Health's biennial congress was being held in Salzburg, Austria. Dick and a colleague decided to attend and see the sights of Northern Europe while they were there. "I'd never been out of the U.S. before," Dick said. "We went to seven countries. Being exposed to other cultures was exhilarating. I felt the same about the World Congress. There were representatives there from all over the world."

Two years later, Dick took his second trip abroad to attend the 1981 World Congress in Manila. What happened next was serendipitous. The newly elected president of the World Federation happened to be from Baltimore, the next congress was to be held in Washington, D.C., and Dick was situated in Virginia, right across the Potomac. "I volunteered to assist the new president with the planning for the congress. It would give me an opportunity to try out my skills in a different arena," Dick said. His offer was gratefully accepted. Dick retired from NMHA and the following day began working on the plans for the upcoming congress.

Since then (1982), Dick has dressed every day in a suit and tie to volunteer full-time for the World Federation for Mental Health. He drives sixteen miles in the congested beltway traffic encircling Washington from his home in Falls Church to the office in Alexandria. Early on, he was named deputy secretary-general and manager of the organization, still as a volunteer.

The mission of the World Federation for Mental Health (of which Margaret Mead was once president) is to promote, among all people, mental health in its broadest terms. Dick's work has been devoted to conceiving ideas and bringing programs to fruition to improve the care and treatment of the mentally ill worldwide. He coordinates each biennial congress, traveling to potential conference sites in-between to assess their suitability. Dick attends the congress itself and board meetings held around the globe, and communicates daily with people all over the world.

When I asked Dick what's been good about this kind of retirement, he smiled. "For all my senior years, I've had the extreme privilege of looking forward each day instead of looking back. It has kept me alive."

He continued. "Mental health is vitally important to me. All my life, my focus has been on accomplishing social change. When I went to law school, I thought I'd do it as a lawyer. Then during World War II, I was drafted as a conscientious objector and sent to work on the wards in mental hospitals. I saw firsthand the abysmal treatment of those with mental illness. I knew then that instead of the law, I would commit my social-change efforts to improving the care and treatment of those with mental illness."

"As a widower, I've had the freedom to devote myself with single-minded focus to a cause to which I'm deeply committed," Dick said. The big payoff for him has been the continued use of his skills and the opportunity to see the world. Dick has now traveled to thirty-five countries. "Mind you, I haven't had the opportunity to be a tourist in all those places," he said. Still, what motivates him is operating in a larger world orbit; having close connections with people in other cultures; knowing that when he goes to Venice, for example, it's because somebody wants him there. "That's a kick. That feels significant."

Dick has worked with First Lady Rosalyn Carter and Second Lady Tipper Gore, the noted psychiatrist, William Menninger, and other key figures in psychiatry. People refer to Dick as the person who started World Mental Health Day, now observed annually in more than 120 countries. The International Committee of Women Leaders for Mental Health was formed at Dick's suggestion and is now operated through the Carter Center in Atlanta. And all of this began after age sixty-eight.

Dick has books stacked everywhere in his home. He reads quite a bit, staying current with the literature in his field, watches television, and is still active in church. "I don't believe in planning one's life too carefully," he said. "All you can do is position yourself for whatever appears. You keep yourself open to the opportunities that present themselves. The people who plan close themselves off from opportunities. Those who decide at fifty that they're going to move to Florida when they're sixty-five, for example, close their minds to other possibilities that might come along in the interim. We need to keep our eyes and ears open and continually prepare ourselves to seize opportunities which appeal to us."

"Don't you ever get tired?" I wondered aloud to my eighty-seven year old friend.

"Sometimes, I'd just as soon stay in bed at seven in the morning, but I get up and go to work. That's where the excitement is," he said.

How do you move from a full-time paid position to a full-time *unpaid* position in your field? "You need to know the organization you want to work with well enough to know what needs to be done. Look for a job that needs to be done and that can't be done except by a volunteer because there's no money to pay for it. It should be a job that everyone would like to have done, and that would give you praise and credit for doing it." He smiled. "Of course, not many people are after your job when you're a full-time volunteer."

Dick's thoughts on retirement? "Everything is discussed as an ending. You *finish* school—an ending term. *Retirement* is an ending term. What's important is what happens next. *Death* is an ending term. Yet we live for what is beyond after death. We need to change our vocabulary," he asserts. "We need to call all these events *commencements*. We need to think of them as *new beginnings*. My years of volunteering with the World Federation for Mental Health have certainly been a new beginning for me."

A SOUTHWEST KITCHEN

"Our kids were away at college and would call home—'Mom, how do you cook so-and-so?' They did it so often that a few years ago, Harry and I decided to surprise our children with recipes for Christmas."

Growing up one of twelve children during the Depression, Adela Amador, seventy-five, of Albuquerque, New Mexico, had learned to cook the simple foods of northern New Mexico. All the meals of the Amador household were built around beans, chile, rice, squash and corn, and a wonderful combination of Mexican, Indian and Spanish flavors.

"Our kids loved the recipes; they're easy and inexpensive. They wanted to give copies to their friends. So my husband, Harry (Willson), a writer and a publisher, and I came up with the idea of putting twelve recipes in a little booklet, calling it *Twelve Gifts—Recipes from a Southwest Kitchen*, printing four thousand copies, and seeing what would happen."

Adela and Harry placed the booklets in independent bookstores around town. At $4 apiece, they were sold in no time. "We were amazed. I guess they made good stocking stuffers or gifts for teachers—that kind of thing. So a year later we printed four thousand more copies, and a couple years after that, four thousand more.

"Early in the process, Harry had tried to get the editor of *New Mexico* magazine to review the booklet. The magazine features stories of New Mexico's people and culture. But they hadn't been interested.

"Then unexpectedly, a year later, the editor of the magazine called and said to Harry, 'We want Adela to call us. We want her to write a monthly column!' They asked me to go to Santa Fe to talk with them.

"When we arrived, the board asked me all kinds of questions about Placitas, where I grew up. They wanted me to write a folksy column about the southwest and about learning how to cook as a child. They were pleased to learn I'd written some short stories published by the University of New Mexico while I was a student there a few years back. We left with their parting words ringing in my ears—'Send us one thousand words for next month, and make it folksy.'

"My first column was for the January issue, so I started thinking about my childhood and our traditional New Year's customs. I wrote about the young fellows of our village serenading us with *Las Mananitas* (a kind of happy birthday song), making *posole* (a traditional New Year's dish made of specially treated corn), and other things from my young life. As month after month went by, with a new column due every thirty days, I was thankful I had a lot of siblings and could ask them what they remembered. It's amazing what I've learned about Placitas, myself and my life as I write. In my column, I often make comparisons between the past and the present, and there's always a point to the story. They're not just ramblings.

"The column changed my life. I've had a custom drapery business for many years. But writing takes a great deal of my time, so in 2001, I turned over the actual sewing to others. Nowadays, I consult and take care of the business end."

Adela's column has brought requests from groups around the state for her to speak about New Mexican history and southwestern cooking. "I tell stories of the pyramids of Mexico, Carlsbad Caverns and the caverns of Spain, my trips to other parts of the world and how what I see connects to our culture."

Recently, the Tourism Bureau of New Mexico sponsored a series of two-minute cooking lessons on public television by Adela and Karlos Baca, a chef at El Pinto, one of Albuquerque's most famous restaurants.

New Mexico magazine polls it's readers annually to get feedback on the success of the magazine. In recent years, readers have consistently voted Adela's column their favorite feature. In 2000, the magazine published Adela's full-length cookbook, *Southwest Flavor*, the name of the monthly column. It has gone into its second printing.

"I love every day," Adela said. "In the mornings, Harry and I have breakfast and do *tai chi* and then I go to the office, work on drapery business, consult with customers, read and write. Sometimes I get calls about recipes. Reading and writing have become more difficult since macular degeneration was discovered in my left eye. It caused a detached retina and I lost my sight in that eye. Now I use a magnifying device, and do all my reading and writing at the shop. I come home by two o'clock and Harry and I play a word game—fighting off Alzheimer's, you know. And we talk. Harry has his writing and publishing. I have the drapery business and my column and my memoirs. And I've written another book: *Undercurrents: New Mexico Stories—Then and Now*. We both have lots of things to talk about."

"There may be others around the country who have a cooking specialty who'd like to write a food column," I said. "What advice would you give them?"

"Well, first it's important to know somebody—somebody who can get your ideas in front of the right people. Second, write about what you know, and start with small and inexpensive recipes. Write everyday, so that you get in the habit. Once your writing is complete, you'll need to find an editor."

Adela's feelings about retirement?

"We have a wonderful life," Adela replied. "I don't think people should retire—not completely. Especially men—they sit in front of the TV, become bored and die early. Find something to do—not some piddling little thing. Be serious, as if you had forever and were going to live another lifetime. Think deep. What do you want? What do you want to do for the rest of your life? If you haven't finished college, go to school and get a degree. I finished my degree in 1974 when I was forty-seven. It gives you confidence you wouldn't have otherwise."

"Adela, can you believe all this happened to you since age sixty-four—all because you're a good cook and your kids wanted you to share your recipes?" I asked. "The newspapers have written feature articles about you, you're on television, you have speaking engagements, and every month your column appears in a national magazine. You're famous!"

Adela laughed. "Honey, it's been a great new adventure."

STAN'S STORY

Imagine being placed in an orphanage as an infant. At age three, you're sent to live with a foster family. Even in Brooklyn winters, your bed is on an unheated front porch. You're fed little and beaten regularly. To survive, you steal little nibbles of food from the refrigerator at night when everyone's asleep—not enough to be discovered— just little tidbits around the edges. At age ten, you beg your social worker to let you go back to the orphanage where you can be with other children. You no longer trust adults.

Even in the orphanage, you're beaten regularly, this time by an older boy. At age fifteen, when a coach swings to hit you, you grab his arm and warn, "Don't hit me, because I'll kill you." With that, you're given the choice of a detention center or being released to the streets. You choose the streets. With $20 in your pocket, you're set free.

Such was the childhood of Stan Appelbaum. One thing was uppermost in his mind when he left the orphanage: he never wanted anyone or anything to control his life again. On the streets of Harlem, he rendezvoused with other teenagers who'd also left the orphanage, only to find them strung out on heroin.

He could see that their lives were controlled by the drug, so he left them and set off on his own.

"I can't think of a single adult who inspired me or urged me on," said Stan. "But I got a job in construction and enrolled full-time at the City College of New York (CCNY), a free university at that time. I finished college, got married when I was twenty, had two children, and a successful career. I was senior vice president of Robert Hall clothing when I left them in my forties to start my own business. My marriage ended when I was fifty. Later, when I was fifty-six, Cathy and I got married and we moved to Bonita Springs, Florida."

Stan and Cathy were like a lot of people who retire to Florida. For the first two years they played golf. But it got boring after awhile. So they started looking around for something to do.

"I decided to become a Guardian Ad Litem, a guardian of a foster child," Stan continued. "Every state has them. In Florida, Guardian Ad Litems go through thirty hours of instruction initially. They also get regular in-service training each year learning how to deal with the court system and how to advocate for the child.

"Guardians go to the foster homes, meet with the children two or three times a month, and attend school meetings," he continued. "They're present at all hearings for the child and make specific recommendations to the court about the child's welfare. During the five years I was a Guardian Ad Litem, I was an advocate for twelve children.

"The case load of the Florida courts is so backed up that our governor has set up Citizen Foster Care Review Boards to act in the place of the Circuit Court. I'm on one of these five-person boards. We meet twice a month to review the status of foster children within our jurisdiction. We decide whether the child can go home, must return to foster care, or if parental rights are to be terminated. Our reviews last up to ninety minutes and everyone's there—the child, the foster family, therapists, the parents, attorneys, the case worker, and the Guardian Ad Litem."

Seventy-five percent of foster children in Florida are in therapy or live in therapeutic foster homes. Therapeutic foster parents have had special instruction in dealing with children with severe emotional problems. Five years ago, the governor appointed Stan to chair the local Florida Mental Health Advocacy Council. This is a huge volunteer job. The advocacy council oversees all agencies funded or licensed by the state that provide mental health services to the citizens of their area. That includes all foster children in therapy or in therapeutic foster care. Stan pointed to his phone. "I have about three hundred numbers on my speed dial, and probably one hundred numbers on my cell phone. My phone is always ringing. Last summer I had prostate cancer, so I've had to change my work patterns to deal with that. Now I work two days a week in the office, and hold meetings and do the rest of my work at home.

"Two years ago two friends and I formed a 501(c)3 organization, the Foster Care Council of Southwest Florida. Our purpose is to enrich the lives of foster children in our five-county area. Foster kids never have more than the basics, you know. So now when a foster child shows an inclination toward art, for example, we see that art lessons and supplies are provided. Or if a child wants to be in the school band, we provide the instrument. We send a lot of kids to summer camp, and we buy clothing—lots of clothing. Last year, we served close to three hundred kids; this year our aim is one thousand."

Stan's organization is growing. They've got eighteen people on the board, twenty volunteers, and a part-time PR person. They held their first fund-raiser during the fall of 2000. Their golf tournament raised $15,000; later that year, they flew in Hollywood comedians for their comedy gala and netted $48,000.

"We've started applying for grants. Last year, three of the four grants we applied for came through. And private citizens provide donations, too. Our first year's fundraising efforts raised fifteen thousand dollars. Last year, we raised one hundred thousand dollars. Our goal this year is two hundred thousand dollars. I work on the foundation at night and on weekends, and Cathy works on it practically full time. It's a labor of love," said Stan, "and because of the support of the community, we've had wonderful success."

"Would you encourage others to get involved with foster child work?" I asked.

"There's such a tremendous need regarding foster children, I wouldn't discourage them. Here, the foster child population has doubled, and there's been no increase in children's services in twelve years. If people are thinking about getting into this kind of volunteer work, they must love children, and have a serious concern for others. But I'd tell them not to do it unless they have a strong affinity for dealing with crisis, intensity and a lot of human emotion. They'll need to be prepared to fight. I guess I'd recommend they start as a Guardian Ad Litem. There's really not a mild way of getting involved.

"Stan, this is such tough work," I remarked. "Surely, it stirs up old memories."

He nodded. "Years ago, when I was getting my divorce, a therapist told me anger was a good emotion if it was used constructively. It has lots of energy. I never forgot that. Doing this work gives me purpose. Who better than I to do it? It matters to the kids when I tell them I was a foster child."

Stan leaned forward. "You know, I see people come to Florida and make their lives golfing or boating and going to early-bird dinners. We did that for awhile, too, but it seemed like such a waste. I think everyone has an obligation to give back by the time they've gotten this far in life. And it doesn't have to be with children. All kinds of people need our help. There are positions open on lots of boards. Just look in the volunteer section of your local paper."

At age seventy-one, Stan hasn't run out of dreams. "My dream is to open a residential home for two hundred foster children within the next couple of years. I'll need two or three million dollars to make that happen, but I think its possible.

This is a wealthy area of Florida and many people are looking for ways to help."

Stan's faced and conquered many challenges in his life. I bet he'll conquer this one, too.

Mel Nowland, Gene Clark
Oklahoma Upgrades

Peggy Day
Peggy Jean's Pies

Joe Walton & local TV personality
Football's the Thing

Helen Lillich
The Tree Lady of West Lafayette

Jeannette Kyllonen, Jerry Engle
The White Coats Are Coming!

Herb McKittrick
The White Coats Are Coming!

90

Sue Turk, Mike Turk, Millie Finkel
Sweetpea and Buttercup—Millie's Happy Times

Richard Busch
Richard's Magnificent Obsession

Jim and Betty Claypool
The New Mexico Dreamcatcher Project

Dreamcatchers
are American Indian
symbols of good luck.

Dreamcatcher card

Merwin Hans
Rural Heritage at Its Best

Mike and Sue Turk
Sweetpea & Buttercup

Arnold Siegel
Soup's On!

Charles Hamblin
A Kentucky Craftsman

Beverly Cullen
On the Way to Genealogy

Autry Brown
The Answer to a Prayer

Pat Smith
For the Birds

Rodney & Kathy Kling
World Explorers

98

Dick Hunter
Around the World in Twenty Years

Adela Amador
A Southwest Kitchen

Stan Appelbaum
Stan's Story

Mary Ann Fontana
Here's to My Ladies

Tom & Mimi Skilling
The Chatham Café

Malcolm Peplow
So Many Adventures

Joanne Hobbs
The Homestead B&B

Dick Bierly
Minding the Shore

Mary Ann Schreit
A Monument to Greene County

Greene County courthouse
A Monument to Greene County

Dick Schiller
Gone Fishin'

George Pucine
George's First Love

Bob and Sally Ambrose
Ridgeview Acres Farm

Moe Steelman
Moe's Legacy

Donna Berg
Paso Robles Youth Arts Center

Paso Robles Youth Arts Center

Bobby Enwright
Bobby and Friends

Elvira
Bobby and Friends

Bruce Valesco
Unity Shoppe

Sofie Minzel, Jane Sprang
Unity Shoppe

Leo Neff
A Second Chance

LeAnn Word
An Artist, At Last!

Gwen and Jake Jolliff
A Retail Adventure

Monty Justice
Monty's Joy Juice®

Margaret More
Music for Minors

Steve Keiley
Foxfire

Evangeline Cothren
Scholarships for All

112

Peter Gregory and horse
Mill Creek Farm

Ken Pasmanick
Music and Musings with the NSO

HERE'S TO MY LADIES

In her heyday, Mary Ann Fontana was singing in Las Vegas, New York, Miami and L.A. An Elizabeth Taylor look-alike, she dated Jackie Gleason and Mel Torme, and was a hat check girl at El Morocco. Until recently, Mary Ann sang at concerts and private parties. "It was my life, and I loved it," she remarked. "Oh, the stories I could tell." With that, she broke into the first few bars of 'I'm in Love with You, Honey.'

"I married two great jazz pianists, had three daughters, and always felt I had to live in Las Vegas. Finally moved here for good when I was sixty. This town is alive with great music and some of the best musicians anywhere. It's show business."

When her best friend died, Mary Ann decided she had to find something to keep depression from taking over. She knew she couldn't give a whole day because of her arthritis, but though she'd like to do volunteer work. She inquired at Catholic Charities and discovered that she could even supplement her income somewhat by becoming a Senior Companion.

The Senior Companion program exists throughout the country to assist seniors in remaining independent in their homes. "There are several kinds of Senior Companion work. You can clean, shop, fix meals, etc. I'm a driver. Four hours a day, Monday through Friday, I take my ladies to doctor and dentist appointments, grocery shopping, to the mall, sometimes to lunch. And we talk and talk. I tell them all my stories about show business—believe me, I have a few—and they tell me about their lives. I learn something new from them everyday.

"My Monday lady is eighty-eight and can't see too well but she's as sharp as you or I. My Tuesday lady is ninety-two. I've been with her for three years. She was the costume lady for a very famous act we all know. My Wednesday lady is ninety-two and has traveled all over the world. My Thursday lady is almost totally blind and doesn't have another soul in the world. And my Friday lady is eighty-nine, moved here to be with her two sons, and they died within a year of each other. I drive them around wherever they need to go, sit and talk with them, and carry bundles into their homes.

"I once had a forty-one year old blind woman. Her mother and sisters live right here in town and don't pay any attention to her. Another time I had the nastiest woman I've ever encountered. She was verbally abusive to me and I took it for over a year. Finally, I told my boss that I didn't want this, I didn't need this, and I didn't deserve this anymore.

"Almost always, these women have no family or else a family that ignores them. I get very close to my ladies. If I can bring them four hours of closeness or happiness, that's what I want to do. I think of my mother. When she was in a nursing home, she always cried when I left. I have great empathy for older people, especially those in need or who are lonely.

"This job gives me a reason to get up and go. It keeps me alert. Last year, I put a hundred miles a week on my car. There are over one hundred Senior Companions in our program here, all over sixty-five. We have big luncheons throughout the year. We receive a small stipend for our work and car mileage of roughly twenty cents a mile."

"The downside to the job is that there's a lot of paperwork. I have to keep track of where I go, at what time, my mileage, and each daily log must be signed by the lady I'm with. Every year I have to have a physical exam, and a checkup on my car to make sure it's up to par. I have 160 days of sick leave accumulated because I hate to disappoint them and take a day off.

"I like what I'm doing. Sometimes I sing," and she broke into "St. Louis Blues." "When I was young and working in night clubs, older women always sought me out—'Come have dinner with me,' they'd say. They talked to me.

"I've met people from all walks of life, people who have lived all over the world, people who once upon a time had money. My ladies always hug and kiss me. They see me wearing jewelry and makeup and now they wear some, too. With a few rare exceptions, all my ladies have been wonderful."

When I asked Mary Ann what she thought of retirement she said, "You better have a plan. And a back-up plan. And you better have money. Retirement is a time to do what you want, but you can't do that without money. Figure out what's fun for you. What gets to your heart? What's important to you? Then go do it."

The Senior Companion program is one of three national programs under the umbrella of Senior Corps, a national network of projects that place older adults in volunteer assignments in the community. Funded through the Corporation for National and Community Service, Senior Corps has existed for thirty years. Mary Ann has been honored with awards for her outstanding service.

"I wouldn't want any other job," Mary Ann said "This is just right for me. And of course, I'll sing for anyone at the drop of a hat."

THE CHATHAM CAFÉ

"Neither of us ever worked so hard in our lives," they exclaimed. "Our bodies ached. We used gallon jugs of liniment to soothe our pain. Between us, we lost thirty-five pounds."

Tom and Mimi Skilling moved from Ohio to retire in Cape Cod. Tom, age sixty-three, had lost the previous year to prostate cancer treatments. It had been a tough time, and they were ready to move on. Both found the idea of milder winters, prettier skies, and the ocean appealing. They weren't sure what they'd do, but they wanted to do something together—maybe open a seasonal business.

Realtors took them to see a bakery, a pie shop, an athletic club, and several restaurants. They were enamored with the idea of taking a small, manageable product and improving it, not buying a product already finished. The restaurant Tom and Mimi eventually bought was exactly what they were looking for. It was small, clean and the rent from two apartments on the property could pay the mortgage.

Both of them had previously owned retail businesses, but they had never owned a restaurant, and never undertaken a venture together. Tom had been a pilot with a major airline for thirty years; Mimi, a clinical psychologist. They met in their forties and this was the second marriage for both.

They bought their restaurant, named it The Chatham Café, and jumped in. They read books, and attended wine tastings and food shows where food products, kitchen equipment, and restaurant paraphernalia were exhibited. "You can taste thirty different lobster bisques, if you choose," Mimi said. They learned about menu price setting and dealing with food distributors. They joined the state restaurant association. They advertised in Cape Cod vacation booklets, with restaurants.com, and in the newspaper, and joined the Chamber of Commerce. County officials inspected the building for fire and health, approved their sign, issued a liquor license and granted safe food handling certification.

They hired a breakfast cook, an evening chef (they're not open for lunch) and two servers—all professionals in the business. "We knew nothing," Mimi asserted. "We had no dishwasher, no salad maker, no dessert maker, no food shopper. We did it all. Our restaurant holds thirty people. The first morning that 147 showed up for breakfast was a three-ring circus. We flew into action." Mimi covered the front, Tom assisted the cook. "Amazingly, only a couple of minor glitches occurred, and no customers left mad."

That is how a working style for the two of them evolved, capitalizing on their individual strengths and inclinations. Mimi's the people person, and Tom loves working with food. Mimi keeps smooth relations with their staff and deals with diners. Tom works in the kitchen and handles business with advertisers, suppliers, county boards, and others in the community.

The tourist season at the Cape is from May through October. That first year of knowing nothing was a great teacher. "Our staff ran the place," Tom acknowledged. "We didn't know enough to do it ourselves. But eventually, we learned the business. We learned how much help we needed. We had employees who worked one shift with us and the other with another restaurant in town. We decided not to do that the next year. Now our staff work double shifts for us in July and August when we're busiest."

Spoilage is a big issue for restaurant owners. Luckily, the Skillings didn't buy excess food very often that first year. Eventually, they learned that their ingredients needed to apply to several dishes. They discovered that their breakfast process was too slow. Now with Tom in the kitchen and two breakfast servers, that problem has been solved.

The second year in operation, their business doubled. They had sufficient dedicated staff. They redid their menu to use ingredients more efficiently, added specials, and expanded their wine list. "It's still a challenge to stay profitable," Tom said, "but that's pretty common in the first few years with a restaurant."

"We didn't lose weight this year," Mimi said, smiling.

"What's fun about all this work?" I asked.

"The challenge is fun," they replied simultaneously.

"When you serve good food with gracious service to 120 people each meal, that is immensely satisfying," Tom said. "We get compliments day in and day out. The first year, we didn't believe them because we felt like such novices."

"Our chef is wonderful and takes great pride in his cooking," Mimi continued. And Tom and Mimi's pride in their business is evident as well. "It's fun to see the astonished looks we get when people find we're new to the restaurant business. It's fun to know that hotels and B&Bs are recommending us to guests. When people exclaim, 'Wow! You own the Chatham Café?!'—that's rewarding."

"What do you think of retirement?" I asked.

"Don't retire!" they replied.

"Forced retirement, as the airlines do with pilots, is not a good thing," Tom continued. "Having no choice was degrading. I was at the top of my game, and I felt cheated. That next year after I stopped flying, I tried a little bit of this, a little bit of that, and sat around a lot. And then I got cancer." He leaned forward. "I'm convinced that if you sit around, you die. Your body gets weak. Your mind gets sluggish. You have nothing to talk about. You're not doing anything!"

"We'll always be doing something, "Mimi added. "I'll die working because I can't imagine the boredom otherwise."

Advice for others contemplating the restaurant business?

1. Be clear about what your concept of having a restaurant is all about.
2. Articulate your standards. Know what you'll accept and what you won't.
3. Be open and flexible. We didn't imagine serving breakfast, but breakfast pays the bills.
4. Location, location, location.
5. If you decide on a seasonal business, as we did, remember it has to pay for the entire year.
6. Be prepared to work as hard as you've ever worked in your life.
7. Be prepared to be there constantly. You can't leave it to your staff to run the place.
8. Read. We found *The Restaurant Manager's Handbook* and *Cooking Essentials for the New Professional Chef* to be helpful.

"Will you do this forever?" I asked, as we ended the interview.

"No," they replied. "We'll do this for awhile. But, this isn't the end. We'll do other things."

SO MANY ADVENTURES

He had just returned home from Thailand, and Malcolm Peplow, seventy-two, of Carnegie, Pennsylvania, had only nineteen days until his next assignment—this time, Jordan. I felt fortunate to meet with him during his brief stay stateside. Malcolm couldn't say enough good things about Thailand. "The Thai people are so gracious and kind. The assignment was interesting, and we stayed in a five-star hotel during our entire visit. My wife, Gloria, and I can't wait to go back. We're hoping for January."

Such is the life that Malcolm has enthusiastically embraced. After retirement in 1986, he did private human resources (HR) consulting for companies in Pittsburgh, Washington and West Africa for several years. But he was ready for a change. What he'd been doing just felt like the same old thing.

Then one day he read an article in AARP's *Modern Maturity* about volunteer opportunities with the International Executive Service Corporation (IESC). Established by David Rockefeller in 1964, IESC's purpose is to assist in strengthening private companies and governments in developing countries, thereby contributing to global stability. In any given year, IESC deploys approximately one thousand consultants worldwide. Malcolm had traveled extensively before retiring and knew he enjoyed exposure to other cultures. He decided to send in his resume, and soon after was interviewed by a local IESC representative.

"My first assignment was to provide HR consulting to what was then the largest company in Yemen, in the Arab Republic. They had the most modern equipment, five thousand employees, and 80-90 percent annual turnover! They had forgotten about the people. So my job was to help them understand that people were their most important asset, and to set in place HR policies and procedures that would reflect this respect for their workforce. I felt I'd done something meaningful by the time I came home from that month-long assignment.

"Another one of my first trips was to Russia," Malcolm continued. "I spent an intensive week in Stamford, Connecticut, at IESC headquarters, being indoctrinated to Russian culture. Then I was assigned to work in southern Russia at it's oldest glass factory. Following that, I went to Kislovodsk, a place where all the czars once went for the spas, and worked for a magnificent entertainment complex there—restaurant, casino, hotel and spa. Assignments are so varied: some in sparse, bleak conditions, others in sumptuous surroundings. You never know what company you might go to next, or what conditions you'll encounter. That's part of the adventure.

"In 1998, IESC asked me to develop a two-day HR seminar to be given in Alexandria, Egypt. When I finished designing it, I presented it to representatives from 138 companies. That exposure brought three more assignments in Egypt, and I gave the seminar in Cairo to another 120 business leaders. We were in Egypt three and a half months. After that, Gloria and I made four more trips to Alexandria and Cairo, three and four months each from 1998 to 2001. IESC will pay for your spouse's travel, as well as your own, so Gloria always goes with me. Your spouse's 100 percent support is essential in this kind of work.

"In 2001, we were supposed to go to Jordan on September 12, but because no planes were flying after 9/11, we left on September 17. During our first visit in Jordan, I was guest speaker at the Jordan

American Business Association, and also put on my two-day seminar for business leaders there. A short time later, we went back to Amman for a month where I worked with an information technology company and an engineering company. During our last trip to Jordan this year, I put together an HR model for the Ministry of Industry and Trade, and then had a four-week assignment with a garment manufacturer.

"It is wonderful to work with people who are eager to learn. Every assignment is a challenge. I don't know the people and don't know their industry. But HR needs are common across the board. I get excited to think that employees may now be treated fairly and that I may have had an impact on the thinking of managers."

The downside? Malcolm says traveling is the downside. The developing countries in which he has worked are a long way away, and the plane rides in coach are very long. Then too, he doesn't know in advance where he'll be living, and some quarters are quite basic. "But today we got email from folks in Thailand and Jordan. You wouldn't believe the emails of condolence we received after September 11. These are the things that make it all worthwhile. It's rewarding to make friends all over the world, and for us, that outweighs the downside."

Malcolm offers the following advice to those who might like to do international consulting:

1. You've got to be 100 percent fit or forget it.
2. You need an adventurous attitude.
3. Talk with other IESC volunteers about the country to which you'll be deployed. They'll help you understand what you're getting into. If you've traveled to other developing countries, you'll understand better the circumstances you may encounter.
4. Be prepared to be flexible, patient and willing to learn. You want to respect your clients and their traditions.
5. Put together a resume. Don't forget to include any international experience you may have had.

Malcolm says he doesn't think of himself as retired. "I've been on a faster pace in the past four years since Gloria retired than I ever was before. I feel I've accomplished more in four years than most accomplish in ten. I've been known as a workaholic, but I feel these jobs keeps me young. This work forces me to think in new ways. I like that.

"Don't consider retirement as the do-nothing time," he continued. "It can be the most challenging and rewarding time of your life. Don't dwell on your past, regardless of what you did. It *is* the past. Figure out how you're going to make the best of this new time. You are about to change your life.

"You'll need to learn to live with your spouse twenty-four hours a day. Fortunately for us, we both love travel and golf, so we have our hobbies in common.

"You know what keeps a person young?" asked Malcolm, as we ended our interview. "It's enjoying what you're doing. So figure out what you love to do and once you retire, go do it."

THE HOMESTEAD B&B

"When my husband died, I slept for three years," said Joanne Hobbs of Bardstown, Kentucky. "We'd had such a good time during the eleven years we were together. We'd been high school sweethearts who married other people and much later, in our forties, reunited. I didn't know what to do when Don died. Finally I realized there was only one person who could make my life full again, and that was me. I thought I might travel for awhile—go back to Texas and see friends, travel around Kentucky a little—but that seemed boring.

"Then one day, I was driving down the road and saw a 'for sale' sign out in front of a farmhouse. When I got out of the car to look closer, there was something about the place that just felt like I was home. My realtor said, 'Oh Joanne, you don't want to see that. It's a mess.' But I did want to see it. I could just imagine what it would look like fixed up. At the time, I had no idea it was a log house because it was all plastered over.

"On June 8, 1997, I bought myself a birthday present. I was sixty-three."

Joanne hired contractors to help refurbish the house and they quickly discovered what lay beneath—a fully intact log house made of tulip poplar, the state tree of Kentucky. Bugs

and termites won't touch tulip poplar. Joanne decided she had
to restore it. "I had a friend who owned a log house and he
promised to help me."

Thus began a three-year restoration adventure. All the
neighbors from the area were excited too, once they found out
about the log house. It was a mess. No one had lived there for
twenty years except the snakes, racoons and possum who were
at home under the eaves. Joanne decided to move in anyway,
even with all those creatures, since she'd begun moving her
things into the house and was afraid of theft.

There was a big old wood stove that didn't quite heat the
house in the room where Joanne was mainly going to live during
the restoration. "I either burned up or froze. You needed a wrench
to turn the faucets on and off. But I'd made up my mind to stay
there. I closed all the doors to the rooms and put my boxed
things in the sun room, with my bed in the dining room. The
first night I got into bed and was almost asleep when there was
a tremendous noise upstairs, running back and forth. I got out
of bed hollering and started pounding on the ceiling to try to
get those critters to quit. And they did."

The first task was the exterior of the house, getting rid of all
the siding and clapboard that had covered the logs. When that
was gone, they could see there was no chink left, the mixture of
sand and cement that served as mortar between the logs. So
new chink was applied. Inside plaster and lathes were removed
from all the walls and ceilings. The floors were refinished and
new hearths were installed. The front part of the house had
been the home of the Nichols family; the back part, their dining
room. "We discovered a slave kitchen behind the dining room.
It took two thousand bricks for the new brick floor we laid in
that kitchen. Upstairs, at the back of the house, were two rooms
for the slaves.

"At first, the craftsman said we couldn't save the slave
kitchen, but I insisted. This room sung to me. So he knocked
out it's ceiling. Now with the huge fireplace, light streaming in

from the windows above, and the beautiful brick floor, it has become the centerpiece of the house.

"We finished in 1999. I invited all the people I'd told I didn't have time to talk to during those years to the Open House. Close to five hundred people came."

Joanne had had a shop out at the farm she shared with Don before she moved to the log house. Once the log house was completed, she opened a shop in it, selling Kentucky country crafts. And in 2001, she opened the B&B. She rents three rooms and adjoining bath.

"My first guests rented all three rooms. They were bikers, in town for the Harley Davidson hog rally. Maybe fifteen hundred motorcyclists descended on Bardstown. I was scared to death and everyone was kidding me about them. But they were the best guests, and one of the couples has been back four times.

"I fix a big country breakfast for my guests—biscuits and gravy, bacon, sliced tomatoes from my garden. Then at 9:30 I start my guided craft tours. I think people should know about Kentucky crafts. I fix a picnic lunch and we visit six craftspeople in the region. There's a lot of talent around here.

"I feel so lucky and so proud that I've saved a little bit of history. Records show that the house was built between 1785 and 1795. Recently the governor deemed it a Kentucky landmark. Next, I'm hoping it will be designated a National Historic Preservation landmark. You have to do a lot of record-searching for that to happen, then fill out the form and send it to Washington. I want that designation so the state won't come in here someday and decide to widen the road and tear the house down."

"Lots of people dream of owning a B&B," I said. "What advice would you offer these would-be innkeepers?"

"I can think of several things to think about:

1. You've got to like people.
2. You've got to be nice and smile all the time.

3. It's difficult if you don't have separate quarters, so think about that.
4. I'm doing this by myself. It would be much easier with another person.
5. Running a B&B is hard; it's a lot of work.
6. Join your state Bed and Breakfast Association. They put out a directory, inspect for sanitation, and give you advice. Then mention your association membership in all your advertising.
7. The Health Department inspects you and checks on smoke detectors, etc. Make sure you understand their requirements. They have helpful advice, too.

"It's been so exciting seeing all of this materialize. Recently, the old Tatum Springs Hotel outside of Chaplin, Kentucky was for sale. That's nearby so I checked it out, but its just too far gone. Once or twice a year I start thinking, "Now what am I going to do?" If something else comes along and I just can't help myself, well . . ."

Joanne loves a challenge. "Even more so, if someone says it can't be done. Not to prove them wrong, but just to see if I can. I have to be doing something, hands on.

"I don't know what retirement is, and I wouldn't really want to retire by myself. I envy people who have someone to do things with—go off on little jaunts. My daughter and I have gone in together on the antiques and crafts that we sell, so she's here from time to time, which is very nice. I do get lonely, though, and I deal with it by staying busy.

"Years ago, someone gave me some advice that I found valuable. It was 'make up your mind what you want to do and then go do it.' But the hardest part is making up your mind. That's what people should work on before they retire—making up their mind."

MINDING THE SHORE

"My wife, Mary, and I retired to Morehead City, North Carolina in 1992 because of the coastal lifestyle," said Dick Bierly, seventy. "The canal adjacent to our home feeds into the inland waterway, the ocean not far beyond. Our boat is moored right at our back door. We enjoy the natural setting, the seabirds and the simple lifestyle. We did a lot of boating and fishing during the first four or five years we were here. The Big Rock Blue Marlin Tournament is held in Morehead City annually with a million-dollar purse and over $100,000 going to charity. It's a big community event and I enjoyed participating and later, being on the board." Life was good.

Then one day, Dick learned that just across from his home on the other side of the canal, developers were planning a marina, twenty-eight boat slips and sixty-five condominiums! To support the development, they were also going to put in a waste treatment plant. Dick and his neighbors were alarmed. They felt the development was not compatible with the community and would have a deleterious impact on their unique setting.

"We formed a community association to try to deal with the situation," Dick said. "We wanted to get to know the

development people, understand what rights we had, what rules
would govern the project, and learn what the ramifications
would be in case we needed to sue.

"North Carolina has specific legislation protecting the
coastal environment and a citizen's group known as the Coastal
Resources Commission (CRC) that writes the rules for
implementing that legislation. Our community group studied
the rules. We made it clear to county officials and Division of
Coastal Management personnel that we expected them to fully
meet the state's requirements for coastal development, the
applicable subdivision ordinances and the land use plan, and
that we'd be holding them accountable. As a result of
negotiations with the trustee of the property, the developers
agreed to build twenty-eight single family homes rather than
the marina, boat slips and condos originally planned—with one
caveat. They asked us not to oppose the property being annexed
to the city because that would allow the new houses to be
hooked to the Morehead City waste treatment system, thus
eliminating the need to build a new one. We were happy to
agree.

"By the time we reached that agreement, I'd learned a lot
about coastal issues and hated to let all that knowledge go to
waste. So I began attending the bi-monthly meetings of the
CRC, and public briefings and hearings held by the North
Carolina Department of the Environment and Natural
Resources. In spite of my intention to keep my mouth shut, I
couldn't resist contributing from time to time. Soon I was asked
to serve on a task force for one group, an advisory board for
another, and various stakeholder groups—all dealing with
coastal environmental issues.

"Five years ago, I became president of Carteret County
Crossroads, a twenty-year-old organization dedicated to
preserving the environment and quality of life in Carteret County
and all coastal North Carolina. We attempt to educate our
membership through newsletters and by conducting open
meetings on important topics. We monitor development

permits. We try to get our elected officials to pay attention to the consequences of their decisions, or the lack thereof, and the impact of unrestrained growth on our environment. We feel the region can have growth *and* a healthy environment if more enlightened guidance governs the development activities. It's not an either/or situation, although many officials and developers present it in those terms.

"Along with other like-minded organizations, we've been able to halt land use planning as it previously existed because it had done little to arrest the steady decline in water quality at the coast and, in its place, form a stakeholder group to revise and streamline the process. Time will tell whether these changes do anything to protect our environment."

Dick and members of his community association often turned to the founder and director of the North Carolina Coastal Federation (NCCF) for advice and direction—probably *the* expert on coastal matters from Virginia to South Carolina. Dick was eventually invited to join their board.

"This is how it evolves," said Dick. "You get started with one thing and that leads to another, and another. If you stay involved, you'll discover what you want to work on and find yourself immersed in activities that can make a real difference. I've been involved with NCCF for four years now."

NCCF has hands-on environmental education programs with middle school teachers and students. In addition, men and women they call coast keepers are out there in their boats, keeping an eye on what's going on along the shoreline and spotting trouble. Volunteers like Dick work diligently to influence North Carolina environmental policy.

"One of the most important things we've done is to form the Coastal Caucus—eight like-minded organizations that meet quarterly. We try to understand what's important to each of us. Our goal is to provide thoughtful input to the state legislature with all of us signing our position papers. We have to compete with trade associations, manufacturers' associations, even municipal government organizations with their well paid lobbyists for attention in the general assembly and governor's office. Tomorrow, I'm going to Raleigh to testify before the Senate Agriculture, Environment and Natural Resources Committee regarding a proposed bill before our general assembly that would relax and undermine the rules of the CRC.

"I think the environmental community does itself a disservice by opposing things. So much of what goes on is biased toward development, and our politicians hide behind their ignorance. My personal efforts have been to educate politicians and anticipate issues so that we can be proactive in our position. I try to work behind the scenes to make things happen."

Dick finds serving on these boards satisfying. "I've always needed to feel useful. If I go to Raleigh to see the lieutenant governor, she gives me a big hug. I guess that makes me feel important. I've learned so much. The experience has been intellectually stimulating."

To get involved in environmental concerns, Dick offers the following suggestions:

1. Join an organization. They need people with organizational and management skills, and people who can speak.
2. Take the time to learn the issues and talk to your politicians. Every state has to deal with storm water runoff and waste water treatment. You needn't have a background in these issues—just the motivation to learn and get involved.
3. You need to be willing to reach out to strangers and learn how to negotiate and compromise.
4. Attend town and committee meetings. All these government issues must be worked out in public. Politicians have a lot of hidden agendas. You won't learn about them unless you're present.

Dick is passionate about his retirement activities and advises all of us to become involved. "Don't get involved occasionally, because you won't feel fulfilled. Find something important to do that gives your life meaning, and dive in. You'll have to reach out and go deeper than just attending Rotary meetings. I have seven grandchildren who live elsewhere whom I don't see as often as I'd like. But I know that if I'm not here for a special hearing when I know I could influence a decision, I feel bad. You let your organization down every time you take off to visit Ireland or go to Florida for the winter.

"I feel like I'm on the side of the angels, working on these issues. You just can't sit back and let unrestrained growth take place without wanting to do something about it. The lifestyle we moved here to enjoy wouldn't be available for very long, if we did."

A MONUMENT TO GREENE COUNTY

Late in the summer of 1992, Mary Ann Schreit, sixty-four, read in a local newspaper that a vote would soon be taken by the Quorum Court to determine whether the old county courthouse would be demolished. It was stunning news to someone who cherished history. The courthouse had stood in the center of Paragould, Arkansas, since 1888 and had once been a grand and majestic building. True, it had seen better days, but surely, something could be done.

Mary Ann began calling friends and acquaintances to see if anyone else was interested in saving the old building. A county attorney and a reporter for the local daily newspaper joined forces with her. The reporter promptly photographed Mary Ann in front of the courthouse, and a few days later, the picture appeared on the front page of the paper with a detailed description of the campaign. The story encouraged those interested in saving the courthouse to call Mary Ann and gave her telephone number.

Within days, several citizens called, and others were recruited. Mary Ann and her group went before the eleven-member Quorum Court that oversees Greene County to inform the court of their desire to preserve the old courthouse. They were advised to return in two weeks to make their case.

"We knew it was essential for people to be able to visualize the restored courthouse," Mary Ann said. "So a local watercolor artist who'd joined our group did a large painting of the courthouse as it had been in its glory days. Then, at the appointed time two weeks later, we appeared before the court with the painting displayed on a large wooden easel and told them, 'We'd like to restore the courthouse to its original grandeur without using a penny of local tax funds.'

"We'd invited the state preservation officer to join us to provide specific information, if needed, in the long session of questions and debate that followed our presentation." Finally, the court voted 6/5 to let the group proceed with the next step: determining if the building was sound and whether they'd be able to arrange financing for the project. They'd need an engineer and an architect and were instructed to come back in one year. The courthouse had been saved by one vote . . . for a year.

"Our next task was to change the perceptions of county residents, most of whom saw the building as a ruined, partially dismantled structure waiting to be leveled for a parking lot. The newspaper showed the watercolor painting on the front page, second section, in full-color so that others could see how the courthouse had looked, and could look again. The reporter kept writing about everything we did in our planning. The newspaper received letters to the editor voicing opinions on both sides of the issue. By then our newer weekly newspaper joined in the campaign with major color coverage and editorials. There was an increase in citizen interest, so we set out to win them to our cause and to raise nine thousand dollars to fund the architect and engineer.

"On Saturday, April 3, 1992, we held a gala 104th birthday party for the courthouse, celebrating the day it was originally completed in 1888. Enlarged prints of the early courthouse were displayed around the grounds, and we sold baked goods and raffled off an Arkansas quilt to raise money.

"For major fund-raising, we called on families far and near and every bank, business, service club, industry and profession. Our original financial estimate for saving the building had been three hundred fifty thousand, but we learned that it would require a lot more to make it a state-of-the-art building. We named ourselves the Greene County Courthouse Preservation Society, elected officers, met monthly, and studied other restorations in the area. We learned of grants we could apply for through the Arkansas Historic Preservation Program and federal subsidies. We incorporated, filed for 501(c)3 tax-exempt status, obtained the services of an attorney, a CPA, and a building architect and soon after, a registered landscape architect."

To keep in touch, members of the group visited the justices on the Quorum Court at regular meetings and were occasionally invited to give an update on their progress. A year later, when they appeared before the court, they placed a six-inch stack of citizen letters asking to save the courthouse at each justice's desk. "Between all the newspaper publicity and our zeal, I think we won them over," Mary Ann said. "The court voted unanimously to allow us to save the courthouse.

"Work began in the summer of 1993, as soon as contracts could be let. In stages, the building began to change. Once the old stucco was stripped away, it revealed twenty-four-inch red brick walls and exterior. The forty feet tall clock tower that had been removed from the building in 1968 was rebuilt on the grounds and hoisted into place by a giant crane before a large crowd and huge publicity in August 1995. Later, chimes were added to the clock to sound the hour, quarter hours and to play seasonal music.

"By 1999, we had raised over $800,000 through private donations, fund-raisers, and grants, and by early 2002 that amount had grown to $1,700,000. We were fortunate that the courthouse was already on the National Register of Historic

Places because that enhanced our efforts to secure state funds, for which there is major competition. Grant applications are incredibly tedious, but we couldn't have done this project without grant money."

The building and grounds have been completely transformed. The first floor of the courthouse interior is furnished like a turn-of-the-century law office—dark-stained period furniture, leather sofas and ceiling fans—juxtaposed with video teleconferencing facilities and high-tech telecommunications equipment. A new elevator and outdoor ramp make the building handicapped accessible. The Chamber of Commerce signed a ninety-nine year lease to occupy the first floor.

"In April 2002, the Arkansas Historical Association held it's annual meeting for the first time in Paragould, with a catered luncheon in the majestic second floor courtroom. This was a very special honor for our city."

Finally, on Friday evening, October 18, 2002, the Chamber of Commerce held a grand reception and ribbon-cutting ceremony showcasing it's new home on the first floor of the courthouse. There were speeches by dignitaries, music and refreshments, tours of the building, and unending thanks to the hundreds of people who donated time, money, in-kind help and professional services. Mary Ann and the other members of the Preservation Society were introduced and honored with personalized plaques.

An even larger celebration will be held in 2004 after completion of the grounds, made possible by a federal byway grant, restoring the town square on which the courthouse is situated.

Although Mary Ann was the original voice of this mammoth project and the Preservation Society's first president, she is quick to tell you that an entire cluster of officers and board members worked tirelessly for this cause.

Nevertheless, for her years of inspiring leadership, Mary Ann received the state's Excellence in Preservation Advocacy Award from the Historic Preservation Alliance of Arkansas at their annual meeting in November 1995.

"Simply put, the courthouse restoration has been one of the most fulfilling experiences of my life," said Mary Ann. "There are other needed restoration projects here and all over the country just waiting for dedicated citizens to take up their cause. For some of those projects, time is running out. I hope many will be saved for future generations."

Mary Ann offers the following suggestions if you, too, would like to be a preservationist:

1. Gather a few like-minded people. You've got to have at least a pair.
2. Find a newspaper reporter/television anchor/editor who will champion your cause.
3. Write letters to the editor and speak to local clubs and groups to rally community support.
4. If you're trying to save a public building, you must win government. Get your building placed on the National Register of Historic Places so that you can receive financial aid for structural repairs.
5. Be courteous. We decided early on never to criticize the Quorum Court. We understood they were coming from a different need.
6. Attitude is powerful. We tried to be diplomatic and generous and maintain a good attitude. We wanted to be open and kind to everyone.
7. Be respectful of each other as a group. Our twenty-five board members differed from time to time, but any disagreements were worked out privately so that they didn't destroy our meetings.

What will Mary Ann do after eleven years immersion in this glorious endeavor, having accomplished such important results? "After a nice rest, and some extra time with my husband and family, I'd like to be of some help in saving the old Pruet house, believed to be the oldest house in Paragould, built by a Civil War veteran who played a major role in the town's founding," Mary Ann said. "Saving that grand old courthouse and getting to know so many wonderful people in the process has been a life-enriching experience. We've truly become friends beyond preservation. Also, we've renewed other friendships from long ago throughout the country by simply getting in touch and asking for support—an unexpected dividend and very great social reward."

GONE FISHIN'

"We were living in England when I retired from Dupont," said Dick Schiller, "and after a few years of traveling around Europe, we settled outside of Louisville, Kentucky, to be near our kids. We live in the country, close to nature. Maybe that's what got us thinking about fishing. Neither of us had fished before but with my wife, Bobbie, going off to basket weaving classes and me heading out to ham radio meetings, we found ourselves going in opposite directions. One day it dawned on us—why not find a hobby we could do together? As we investigated possibilities, fly fishing sounded particularly appealing. We had no idea it would lead to all this," Dick said, glancing around his basement shop.

When Dick and Bobbie took lessons to learn to cast a fly rod, they became particularly interested in trout. "Trout live in cold, clear water, which means we'd have the pleasure of visiting pristine mountain settings or beautiful wilderness areas for our fishing. And trout don't swim around in schools looking for food, as other fish do, which makes them much more challenging to catch.

"The first glorious setting we visited was at the Winston Rod Ranch in Montana where we went for a week-long course in fly fishing. They taught us so much, from the entomology of bugs and aquatic insects, to how to think like a trout. Through our local chapter of Trout Unlimited, an association for trout fishermen, we took several excursions to Yellowstone. We also spent a week at the John C. Campbell Folk Art School in Brasstown, North Carolina, where they offer courses in all sorts of crafts, including tying flies. Flies can be expensive, but after an initial expense for supplies, making them yourself is not, and in the middle of the winter when we're not able to fish, tying flies is a great activity."

About a year after returning from Brasstown, Dick attended a local flea market and struck up a conversation with a man who had a collection of bamboo fly fishing rods. Bamboo fly fishing rods are special because of bamboo's great flexibility and strength. Due to climactic conditions, a type of bamboo (Tonkin) that is perfect for fly rods and unlike any other in the world, grows in a place in China only twenty-five miles square. When the embargo of Chinese goods occurred in the 1950s and access to Tonkin bamboo was cut off, U.S. rod manufacturers began using fiberglass and graphite instead. Today, only four American companies sell bamboo rods as a sideline. Some of them sell for over to $2,500. There are also about four hundred individuals in the U.S. making these rods. Dick decided he had to be one of them.

Dick says it takes forty to sixty hours to make a bamboo rod. It is painstaking work. Thin strips, no more than a quarter inch wide and three to five feet long, are glued together in square or hexagonal shapes forming a rod. Metal guides to hold the line are wrapped on the rod at regular intervals. Dick's basement shop contains stacks of Tonkin bamboo, cork, silk thread, varnish, glue and other raw materials, and many specialty tools to facilitate the gluing and finishing of the rods. The rod handles are made of pieces of cork ordered straight from Portugal. Because bamboo is a natural material, each rod is slightly different, and the fittings and trim make each unique.

"There are Fords in fly rods, and there are Jaguars. I want to make Jaguars," Dick said.

Dick has given away many rods, and he teaches, but doesn't charge. "I don't want the responsibility that comes with selling a product or service. Students come from other states and towns around Kentucky. Right now I'm working with a young banker who lives nearby. We meet twice a week for up to eight hours a session.

"As with most hobbies, there are so many routes you can take. In fly fishing you can make rods, or flies, of jigs, or nets, or baskets. The Internet is the best source in the world to learn about everything. Search rod makers on Google.com and it will direct you to all the rod making sites.

"Bobbie and I have joined rod makers' groups, and now I have a lot of fly fishing friends whom I hear from by email. We've read many books and attended as many classes on rod making, fly tying, and fly fishing. When you have someone to teach you, rather than reading about it, it goes so much faster."

What does Dick think of retirement? "We should be retired until we're fifty-five, and then work—do all these wonderful things while we're young and healthy. Seriously, I think several things are important for retirement:

1. You've got to have a certain amount of money to be able to live in the style to which you are accustomed. Get rid of all big debts first.
2. Have a system for taking care of your health, and adequate medical care.
3. Don't move too far from your family. We enjoy being near our children and grandchildren. They like to see us and we like to see them. We think watching our grandchildren grow is entertaining, relaxing and rewarding.
4. You need a passion. Decide on something you want to

do, and then learn all you can about it. When you've mastered it, you can teach others. It's so important to have something to look forward to. Travel won't cut it for long."

Fly fishing has captured Dick and Bobbie's imagination for several years now, and Dick's skill at making bamboo fly rods has been featured in newspapers around the state. The Kentucky Fish and Wildlife Department produced a video showing Dick making rods which has been shown on local television. Area sporting goods shops send people to him when their fly rods need repairs. And through his instruction, Dick has the pleasure of passing on his knowledge to others. At seventy-five, Dick is doing just what he'd like to be doing.

GEORGE'S FIRST LOVE

When George Pucine was in first grade, he heard music coming from the classroom next door. Curious, he discovered that piano lessons were being offered to anyone in the school who wanted them. George immediately signed up. He loved music and had always enjoyed hearing his grandfather playing his instruments.

Every week, when George arrived for his lesson, the teacher would ask for his payment, and every week George told the teacher he'd forgotten to bring it. Finally, the music teacher called George's parents. "You must be mistaken," George's mother said. "George isn't taking piano lessons. We don't even have a piano." The teacher informed her that not only was George taking lessons, he was her best student! Later, George's mother learned that her ingenious son had 'practiced' on a keyboard printed across the open pages of his school book. It was obvious the family had to get a piano.

George took lessons all through school, and played piano in big bands until he was twenty-eight years old when he got married, moved from New York to California, and began a career in the aerospace industry. Although he dabbled in song writing from time to time and played the grand piano in the living room during occasional family gatherings, music took a back seat to his career and growing family for the next twenty years.

Then in 1984, when George was forty-nine, circumstances led him back to music. When the choral director at his church became ill, a friend who knew of George's musical abilities asked him to take over the direction of the choral group that sang for the 11:00 A.M. service. Every Sunday thereafter until he retired, George led the group for that service, and for weddings, funerals, Memorial Day and Christmas Eve as well.

"I retired at sixty-two in 1995, and my wife, Iris, and I moved to Sun City Summerlin in Las Vegas, Nevada. We wanted an adult community where there'd be lots to do," George said. "Right away, I began singing with two senior groups—the Silvertones with seventy voices, and the Music Makers with forty. We do four-part chorale arrangements and I stage the musical vignettes we perform as part of our spring concert. Both groups rehearse every week and perform in May and December to packed houses at the community theater.

"Déjà vu all over again," George quipped. "A couple of years after I joined the Silvertones, the director became ill and I was asked to take over. I receive a small monthly stipend in exchange for selecting our music, transposing it, arranging for the voices in our group, conducting rehearsals, and working with the sound and lighting people at the community center to stage our productions.

"Our last show was 'A Taste of the Tropics; a Touch of the Blues.' We do songs of the '30s, '40s, and '50s, and are fortunate to have a wonderful jazz piano accompanist. We sing standards, but it's also fun to challenge the singers by introducing songs they haven't sung before."

The song writing George once did occasionally is now a regular activity, and sometimes the choral groups sing his songs. "I spent a year reading everything I could find about composers and song writing, studying composers like Johnny Mercer and Oscar Hammerstein. Then I joined the Las Vegas Songwriters Association, the Northern California Songwriters Association, and the International Songwriters Association. It's important to form a working community with whom to compare notes and critique each other's work. Each association has a monthly magazine chockfull of information—tips on writing, the names and addresses of singers looking for ballads, and upcoming conferences. Music publishers are listed who will provide feedback on your songs, if you mail in recordings of them.

"I gave myself three years to get a song accepted by a publisher. In the third year, I got two songs accepted, and now I have five. Someday, I'd like to turn on the radio and hear one of my songs. That would be such a thrill. Sometimes I've been discouraged. But then I'll hear back from a publisher—'This is a good song, but not what I'm looking for. You have a nice jazzy-bluesy style.' That keeps me going.

"There are courses on song writing, many of them offered by artists whose songs have been recorded. Or you can educate yourself, as I did.

"There's so much you can learn on the Internet. And don't forget to join the associations. They cost anywhere from thirty-five to one hundred twenty-five dollars a year, but they get you in the groove and you begin associating with other song writers.

"If you're interested in choral music, start a group. To organize something like ours, here are some suggestions:

1. Put a notice in your local newspaper. Ask for people who enjoy the songs you are planning to perform (music of the '30s, '40s, and '50s, big band music, etc.)
2. Here in Sun City, the community association requires that any activity have at least thirty people to be sanctioned by it. That seems to be a good starting number. You should also determine how large you want the group to grow.
3. Elect officers and a music committee to work with the director in selecting your music. Make sure these folks are knowledgeable about music. Put the word out in the community that you're looking for a director. You'd be

       surprised how many people there are who used to play and sing, and love music.

4. Decide on what you'll charge for dues to pay for your music and your accompanist. Depending on the size of the group, it could be between thirty-five and seventy dollars per year.

5. Most important, make it fun! I've run into "military police"-type directors before—your group falls apart then. Currently, the Silvertones rehearse for two hours a week without a break, but we have fun as we're doing it. And we don't rehearse during the summer when people are so often away. In September, everyone comes back refreshed and ready to go."

About retirement, George says, "I remember a day in San Jose, before I retired, when I came home from work and saw a neighbor sitting in a rocking chair on his porch. I told Iris I was never going to sit on the porch watching the grass grow, waiting to die.

"I've known people who feel they cut off their left arm when they retired. They had nothing else going on in their lives. They didn't know what to do. Everyone should think about this. If you're going to retire, you need to get into something you've always liked. Find something. Volunteer with AARP—it's a good organization. If you're fortunate enough to have had an avocation, now's your chance. There are lots of courses to take in so many different fields of study."

George is relishing every minute of his return immersion in music. "I love playing. I love singing. I love song writing. I love directing. I was drawn to music in first grade and the pull is just as strong today. I'm living the perfect retirement for me. There's nothing else I'd rather do."

RIDGEVIEW ACRES FARM

Farming hadn't been their profession. Bob was a construction engineer; Sally, a math teacher. But that changed when they retired and moved to the farm in Stahlstown, Pennsylvania.

"We helped my dad for three years before he died," said Bob Ambrose. "He'd thought about selling, but we convinced him otherwise. The farm had been in the family for two hundred years. For many years prior to retiring, we commuted from Cincinnati every other weekend, overseeing the maintenance of the farm." That's how Sally and Bob got into full-time vegetable farming, never suspecting acres of flowers would blossom into their lives.

When they retired and moved to the Pennsylvania farm for good, they began taking their produce to the Ligonier Farmers' Market every Saturday during summer and fall. They'd arrange their stall neatly and colorfully, a vase of some of their homegrown flowers perched on the display for added decoration.

"A turning point came one Saturday when a woman asked about the price of broccoli," Bob continued. "When she heard it was seventy-five cents she remarked, 'I pay that price at the supermarket so there's no point buying it now.' Then she looked at the vase of flowers. 'Those are beautiful. I'll take those. How much?' she asked. We said 'five dollars' and she never blinked. We realized right then we were in the wrong business.

"We weren't ready to give up on vegetables, but we started growing acres of flowers, too. Besides taking them to the farmer's market, we began calling on country clubs, restaurants, B&Bs, grocery stores and florists. Our flowers are not the traditional varieties—carnations, roses and the like. We grow over three hundred varieties of the kinds of flowers you'd find in a cottage garden. It may take a year to convince a florist to use our flowers. They'll buy a little at first, see how they hold up, and get to know us. Little by little, these retail establishments are coming on board.

"Last year, we began selling flowers to wholesale distributors. About ten percent of our business was with them, and this year we're hoping it will be twenty percent."

"So what is your year all about?" I asked. "Starting with January, what do you do?"

Sally responded. "We start planting in our three greenhouses in January. Annuals, some perennials. Some plants have a sixteen-week growing schedule, others twelve weeks. We're planting throughout January, February and March to account for their varying growth cycles and so that everything doesn't bloom at once."

"Generally, in November, we plant the seeds in flats and keep them under special lights in our living room until they've sprouted," Bob continued. "Once they have a couple of true leaves, they're transplanted to larger containers and put in the greenhouse. They stay in those containers until they're sold or replanted outdoors. Transplanting usually occurs in mid-February. They go outdoors in mid-April or beyond. From then on, you're dealing with insects, disease and weeds, and rain or no rain. Six acres. It's a delicate balance."

"We got started with flowers in 1998, but we never cut

back on our vegetables. We didn't plan to get big; it's just happened. Now flowers are over 50 percent of our business.

"We have a pool of five employees throughout the summer—high school and college kids. On Fridays, we try to have everyone here because it's the day before market. Market starts the first weekend in June. The rest of the time, three or four of them are here, depending on their schedules. Ironically, September is our busiest month and all the kids are back in school. So we work longer. Sometimes we go to bed at two in the morning and get up at five thirty or six."

Sally chimed in. "But we bought a huge cooler this spring. That means we don't have to do all our cutting on Friday. We can cut two days ahead and store in the cooler."

"What do you do when the season's over?" I asked.

"We come home from market, put our feet up, and get out the beer," Bob replied. "We still have pumpkins and some of our frost-proof flowers to sell to wholesalers through October, but our season is over by the end of September."

"That's when I go off and play grandma," Sally said. "And then come home and skiing season starts. That was my deal with Bob when we came here. I'd do farming as long as I could be a ski bum during skiing season. Actually, I work in the ski shop on the weekends, and ski the other five days. Bob stays home, combing through seed catalogs. And one day a week he still does construction consulting. In January and February, he also goes to growers' meetings in Maryland and Pennsylvania."

"There's a lot of hard work in what you're doing," I remarked. "What's good about this life you've carved out?"

"We're not bored," Sally replied. "We're outdoors and can enjoy nature. We're learning all the time. We really didn't know much about flowers, and nothing about flower arrangements. Now we do flower arrangements all the time for country clubs, restaurants, even weddings. And we've started drying flowers for arrangements and wreaths. We're providing people with pleasure. They keep coming back and that's satisfying."

To start a vegetable and/or flower business, Sally offers the following insights:

1. Don't go into this thinking you're going to make a significant amount of money. You won't.
2. Staying small may be more profitable than getting large because of the labor costs. Maybe you'd need only a mid-sized greenhouse rather than all three. Our heating bills in the winter run $500 a month with all three.
3. You learn by making mistakes. It's trial and error.
4. You have to be willing to work from sun up to sunset. You will never have a forty-hour week.
5. Make sure this is something you really enjoy. If not, all this work won't be worth it.

Bob's advice:

1. Eighty percent of the population should not own a business because they have no fire in the belly. If you've no fire in the belly, don't try it.
2. Make sure you're adequately capitalized and not going to fold due to lack of money.
3. It's very easy to grow things, and very hard to market.
4. You need strength and stamina for this work.

"You're in your mid-sixties now. What will you do when you get older and your strength and stamina decline?" I asked.

"We're always going to live here," Sally replied. "When we get older, we'll cut back on the annuals—the things that have to be planted every year. Maybe only do spring and fall work, and stay out of the summer heat.

"I love retirement," she continued. "You're able to do what you want to do. It's never boring, you're learning and challenged all the time. I feel sorry for people who don't know what they want to do. We were never that way. Of course, I thought I'd be quilting, but moving here allowed me to be a ski bum. I wanted to meet people to ski with so I started working at the ski resort. You try to get yourself into a situation that will help you do what you want to do."

"You're talking retirement. Who's retired?" Bob asked. "I'm working ten days a week on this, ten hours a week on consulting, and I'm president of the Farmers' Market Association. We have eighty vendors, the largest market in western Pennsylvania. But this is all okay because I don't know how to sit still. A lot of other people's retirements seem sterile, dull and uninteresting to me. They need to do something they love doing.

"We've got a good life," he concluded.

Sally nodded. "No matter how much your body hurts, get up and get moving because if you don't, you'll sit and do nothing."

MOE'S LEGACY

"You're going to reach a point where you want to leave a legacy," remarked Maurice (Moe) Steelman, seventy-one, of Lafayette, Indiana. "Not just your children, but something more intangible." And that's how Moe ended up at the Lafayette Adult Resource Academy (LARA).

A year before he'd retired from Nabisco, Moe and his wife, Jeannine, moved from Gary to Lafayette, Indiana. It seemed like a nice place for retirement because of the university. No longer selling cookies and crackers, Moe dabbled in this and that for the first few years, delivering paint, working in a book store, but he knew he wanted to do some kind of volunteer work.

He'd read about the academy; LARA is devoted to helping adults achieve English literacy. Some students are developmentally challenged, some are working on their General Educational Development (GED), and some are learning English as a second language. Moe began by volunteering one morning and one evening a week, helping adults and juvenile offenders study for their GED. One day, the director of the academy asked Moe if he could work with English as a Second Language (ESL) students. "Could you just have a conversation with them?" she asked.

Moe started out with five foreign graduate students attending Purdue. They can read and write English very well, but speaking it is more difficult. "I told them they could talk about anything, I didn't care what the subject. We could talk about their country, or food, or current events. Slowly, timidly they began talking. We're all like babies as we're learning a foreign language," Moe remarked. "We start off with single words, then 'me cookie,' and later basic sentences. I don't interrupt them. The point is for them to try to put a sentence together."

The strategy worked. Moe dropped his GED tutoring as more and more foreign students began showing up for his ESL conversations. Soon, one night a week became two, then three, and then four. Now, four nights a week from six o'clock until nine, Moe holds conversations. He never knows who will show up, or how many. The academy's only requirement is that students participating in the program attend a minimum of twelve hours a month in order to hold a place in the group.

To keep the conversations interesting, Moe has come up with all sorts of creative approaches. Every month, a political science professor holds a conversation about elections or current events with the group. They've had "celebrity conversations" with the chief of police, the mayor, and the superintendent of schools.

In the summer, Moe organizes a picnic. He's also taken them strawberry picking. "To help them learn about baseball, we played it. To explain Christmas, we had a tree here at the academy and we talked about the ornaments, and the star. We had turkey, and cranberry sauce and eggnog. Twice a year, we have ethnic food tasting. The students love sharing food from their countries. We bought chopsticks and gave lessons in how to use them. So its not just conversation," Moe acknowledged, "its also cultural exchange. I like that."

Moe insists on a round table for the conversations so that everyone is equally involved. "My job is to be a good listener," he said. "Things are going best when I'm sitting back, listening. Once in awhile, the conversation can get a little contentious: Arabs and Jews, China and Taiwan. But my guideline is that we are friends who will part as friends."

Moe loves his work. "Where else can I sit down and talk to people from all over the world? These folks are young, they're bright and they're interesting. They feel comfortable with me. I've been told that my voice is gentle and my demeanor non-threatening. I can't help but think they see me as a father figure.

"Not too long ago, two students from Japan were going home. We had 'farewell' inscribed in Japanese on top of a cake for them. Several times a year, I receive emails from past students who live in Iran, Brazil, Yugoslavia, Korea and Japan. Last week, three new people from Colombia joined the group. So the group membership changes from time to time. I see these conversations as building bridges between their nation and ours.

"Almost every community across the country has ESL instruction, and these programs are always looking for volunteers," said Moe. "If you like young people and have a curiosity about others, you might want to try it. You can start out one-on-one, and then move on to holding group conversation, if that feels more comfortable. And if you keep it interesting and fun, your group will grow."

Moe represents the academy's ESL activities from time to time at meetings held elsewhere in the state. In 1995, he received the J.C. Penney Waterford crystal trophy for Outstanding Volunteer Service to the Community, and in 1996 the Outstanding Tutor Award from the Indiana Literacy Foundation. "It's nice to have your efforts recognized," said Moe. "But what gives me satisfaction is not the recognition but the accomplishment. I didn't realize this when I retired, but those of us who've been employed are used to challenges, interacting with others, and accomplishing something. I wanted to get away from the stress when I retired, but I still want to accomplish something. With the meals I deliver to shut-in seniors in the mornings and this work in the evenings, I think I've done that."

"What advice would you give to others about to retire?" I asked.

"Retirement is great," said Moe, "but people need to think about it ahead of time. Don't think you'll just play golf or watch the garden grow, because you won't be satisfied with that. All of us need to feel we're making a difference.

"You know what I'd love? I'd love to think that one day in a coffee shop in Tokyo or Moscow or Beijing, someone will mention they remember a guy in the United States who helped them once."

PASO ROBLES
YOUTH ARTS CENTER

"When we bought our place just outside of Paso Robles, I had no special retirement plans. My husband, Bob, was still working in LA, but after twenty years as an accountant, I was looking forward to a peaceful time with our animals, away from the city," said Donna Berg, sixty-five. "Then Mother Theresa died. I was so upset I told my husband I had to go to India to help those poor children left behind. A lengthy discussion ensued, and he convinced me I could help children right here at home. That's how it began. Mother Theresa's death was some sort of call to action for me."

Halfway between LA and San Francisco, Paso Robles, California, is a community of twenty thousand nestled in the mountains twenty-five miles east of the Pacific Ocean, vineyards all around. "When I inquired around town about the needs of Paso Robles' children, I learned that a music and arts program was sorely needed now that none was offered in California public schools. There was a small, popular program of tutoring and recreation being offered to children at Oak Park, a low-income housing development in town. But the program had limited funds, and the three trailers used for it were small. I could see where I might help."

Donna discussed her ideas with city officials and then, at her own expense, hired teachers to expand the program at Oak Park. She began by offering free tap and jazz dance instruction six days a week. Later, she hired a director and together with the children, they put on a production of "Oliver," costumes and all. "We had four sold-out nights at $5.00 a ticket! The children and parents loved it. Everyone was excited, and I began imagining even grander possibilities for the program, although it was easy to see our current facilities would be too small."

With two years experience at Oak Park behind her, Donna began looking for a larger place to rent. She thought they needed at least five thousand square feet. Then one day, while driving down the main street of town, she noticed a vacant lot on the corner of Spring Street. It was owned by the city and intended for low-income housing, but Donna saw it as a perfect location for an arts center.

Donna applied for and received a $135,000 grant from the city to be used "to enrich and improve the lives of low income residents." She pleaded with the City Council to let her buy the corner lot so she could build an arts center there. They agreed to sell the land to Donna for $135,000 and, as the new year rang in, she excitedly began preliminary planning with architects.

Then in April 1999, in the midst of working with architects and contractors, Donna was diagnosed with breast cancer after a lump was discovered during a routine doctor's appointment, and quickly underwent a mastectomy. This traumatic and unexpected event required four weeks of recovery, treatment, and physical therapy. The arts center project was temporarily put on hold. "I was worried and fatigued and for awhile found it difficult to concentrate on more than my health. Eventually, I decided I intended to beat this thing and was going on with my plan."

Generous contributions helped finance construction. Donna organized a Hard Hat Ball—a big dinner and auction—held in the unfinished arts center, and raised $45,000. "The Hearst Castle is not far from here," said Donna, "and the Hearst Foundation gave another fifty thousand dollars; the county, twenty-five thousand dollars. Many individuals around town donated. The city gave us sixty-five thousand dollars to help with the sidewalks we'd need to install. We'd budgeted a million dollars for the construction. After the sidewalks and sewers, eight hundred thousand dollars remained for the building. We were fortunate. I told our contractors we were poor, and all of them gave us huge cuts. We ended up coming in two hundred thousand dollars under budget."

A large room was added to the original plans, to be used by the city. In exchange for rent-free use of the room, the city agreed to pay the utilities for the entire building and take care of indoor and outdoor maintenance. Today, the city's room is a children's library and computer classes are taught there.

The grand opening of the beautiful, green-trimmed, grey stucco Paso Robles Youth Arts Center took place in November 2001. City officials, donors, mothers, fathers, their children, and the media attended the ribbon cutting. "It was a glorious event. Unfortunately, it was hard for me to completely enjoy it as I was very, very sick. I'd unknowingly become ill with a bacterial infection while being treated after my mastectomy. From the time we broke ground, shortly after my surgery, I raced down to the construction site every day, meeting with the contractor and making decisions even though I'm not a builder. I was exhausted and not getting much sleep which I attributed to the workload, not an infection. But after the grand opening, I was hospitalized. It took months for me to get back to normal."

Donna showed me around the spacious Arts Center. There's a large, open foyer, an auditorium that can be divided into two dance studios, and the green room behind the stage which is used for keyboard, guitar and voice lessons. The six-hundred-square-feet kitchen doubles as an art studio, and Donna and her assistant have a large office. The parking lot accommodates twenty-six cars.

"Each week we offer dance, drama, music and art classes—thirty-two classes, in all. The classes are free and there is never a charge for costumes and supplies. The kids are wonderful, and I get so much from seeing them and knowing I'm keeping them off the street, off drugs. We're open Monday through Friday after school from 3:00 to 6:00 and from 1:00 to 4:00 each weekday during the summer. I work hard every day on the computer, scanning the kids' artwork, and designing invitations and programs for our events—that sort of thing."

Donna says you don't have to have money to start an arts program in your community. "Robert and I are very fortunate, and had money we wanted to contribute to this project. But if you don't have money, you can use city facilities, conduct fundraising events, and not get quite as carried away." Other advice?

1. You have to have the will and the stamina to do this. It requires day-to-day attention to your program and to your community.
2. Connect with people who know about the kinds of things you want to do. I knew nothing about art or dance.
3. This place makes a difference because we have structured semesters—four semesters, each one eight to ten weeks long. One hundred seventy-five kids are enrolled free each semester. We don't have a problem with absenteeism. The kids love what they're doing, and know we always have a waiting list. We never have to advertise.

"Let's face it, it's a lot easier to do a project like this if you put up a lot of the money yourself. Bob and I have contributed close to $2 million for the building and the foundation that supports it, and we're happy to do it. If you have the money, why not share it?"

"You haven't really stayed home with your animals as you'd imagined, have you?" I asked.

"I couldn't possibly retire without doing something," Donna replied. "Everyone who can should make a difference in this world. Help somebody. It doesn't have to be on this scale. But go for it. You don't need to have everything in place to get started. We started very small at Oak Park, and then expanded. Just jump in and begin!"

As we wrapped up our interview, Donna said, "I can't believe I did this. It was a huge project. I was so fortunate to receive so much encouragement from my husband. Today, my assistant takes care of day-to-day operations; I work on the big-picture issues, and at the computer. It's a joy coming here every day, knowing we're making a difference with the kids of Paso Robles. I never had children of my own. Now, these are my children. What a blessing."

BOBBY AND FRIENDS

Elvira would make the three-hour ride to the Veterans Administration (VA) Medical Center in North Little Rock in the back seat of Bobby Enwright's Plymouth. She was young then—about eighteen months—and enjoyed the change of scenery. Once they arrived and had had a chance to stretch their legs, Elvira would walk with Bobby up the front steps of the hospital where they'd be met at the door by the recreation director, given their visitors' badges, and escorted to the elevator. Just as proud as she could be and without a moment's hesitation, Elvira would step into the elevator for the ride to the third floor. It was great to be a llama, out and about.

"We'd assemble with the ambulatory patients in the activity room," Bobby said. "I'd take Elvira up to each patient so they could pet her or hug her. The people who worked there would line up, too. They wanted to pet Elvira, just like the others. Then the recreation director would take us down the hall and tell us which rooms we could enter. In a couple of hours, we'd leave for the drive home. It's a full day when we go to Little Rock.

"After I retired from the Air Force, I worked for Montgomery Ward in Maryland for awhile," Bobby said. "Several of the

nursing homes in the area had service contracts with us, and I'd
often be called to repair a resident's TV. Many, many times
when I got there, the residents would tell me nothing was wrong.
They just wanted to talk. When I started investigating their
circumstances, I learned that most of these folks didn't have a
single visitor all year. I knew I was going to do something about
that someday."

Bobby grew up on a farm in Iowa and always loved animals.
When he retired for good, he bought forty-two acres in the
Ozark Mountains of northeastern Arkansas and started raising
cows and miniature donkeys. "On my mother's ninetieth birthday
in 1992, I went back to Iowa. She was in a nursing home and I
took Joshua, one of my miniature donkeys, to visit her. I guess
that's what started it all.

"Since then I've taken animals of all kinds to visit senior
centers, skilled nursing facilities, the VA, the Calico Rock
Nursing Home, the library for children's story hour, and vacation
Bible schools. Elvira will go right up to a sick person's bed and
lay her head on it so she can be touched. She seems to sense
that they're ill. No one has to say a thing. One stroke victim
who hadn't moved in three years put out his hand to touch
Elvira."

It takes Bobby the better part of a day to clean Elvira prior
to her visits out into the world. He uses a wire brush. "You can't
use water; you'd end up with a mass of tangles. The animals'
natural oils help clean their coats.

Bobby now has horses, cows, calves, miniature donkeys,
llamas, a rooster, hens, baby chicks, peacocks, and muskogee
ducks. It's a veritable zoo. Each of the llamas and donkeys has
been on therapy visits, except for Torey, the new baby llama.
They all live comfortably together in the same pasture.

"I love animals. I even had a pet deer whose mother had
been killed on the road. I nursed him with a bottle and he lived
here with all the other animals for three years until he went off
one year at mating season and didn't return."

How do you go about raising therapy animals?

"The most important thing is that you've got to socialize your animals from the start. Get them used to strangers, and being touched by people. If you buy an animal, make sure its young—an older one won't bond with you and may not be sociable. Second, you need to enjoy older people if you're going to be involved in this. While your animal is young and once you think you're both ready, call the recreation director wherever you want to go and set up an appointment. They'll want to look over you and your animal. At first, people wanted to see Elvira's shot records. But since the first visit, they haven't asked for them. In some areas of the country, therapy animals have to be temperament-tested, too."

Five years ago, when Bobby was sixty-eight, he was diagnosed with Parkinson's disease. Two years ago, his energy was so low and his shaking so severe that he had to stop his visits with the elderly. But a year later, Bobby started taking a new medication and is doing much better. His energy has returned, his shaking is greatly diminished, and he and his animals have resumed their visits.

"What do you think of retirement, Bobby?" I asked, as we walked back from the pasture.

"I'm a lucky man. Adean and I met in church a year after I was divorced and five years after she'd been widowed. We dated for four months and got married. We've been married four years and have a wonderful life together. We're able to get away two or three times a year by hiring a neighbor to take care of the animals while we're gone. The last ten years have been the best years of my life. I have a wonderful wife, a lovely farm, my animals, good neighbors, a good church. We're blessed."

Bobby's received awards for outstanding volunteer service to the community, newspaper articles have been written about him, and he and Elvira have been featured on *Animal Planet*. But that's not what's important to him.

"It makes me feel good to give a lonely person a little bit of happiness."

UNITY SHOPPE

Unity Shoppe is a unique non-profit organization in Santa Barbara, California. Founded in 1917, it acts as a central distribution facility for 213 non-profit agencies, social service organizations, churches, schools and hospitals. It is the largest distributor of food and clothing to low-income families, the elderly, sick and the disabled in the county of Santa Barbara, distributing over $2.7 million in merchandise yearly. No referral is ever turned away.

Seventy-five percent of those served are working people whose paychecks don't always cover much beyond housing. Unity Shoppe supplements these limited incomes with food, clothing, shampoo, shoes, blankets—even toys. Families may shop with dignity for their needs from the well-stocked shelves of Unity Shoppe's free store. Home- or hospital-bound individuals have their requests delivered to them.

On the first Saturday of every December, the local ABC television station hosts a celebrity-studded "Unity Telethon" to help raise the funding needed. Television and movie stars, musicians, local business people, community members and the children—all pitch in to help those in need. During the year, men, women and children donate or collect funds, food, gifts and clothing as they volunteer their talents to the cause. I was fortunate to meet three of the over six hundred senior volunteers who act as "Good Samaritans" for Unity Shoppe.

Bruce Velasco, seventy-one, was an electronics engineer at General Motors (GM) before retiring, and is one of eighteen GM retirees making wooden toys for Unity Shoppe. "At first, we used only scrap lumber. But now the local lumber yard gives us all the wood we need, and a paint store gives us our paint. Tonka (Toys) gave us ten thousand wheels.

"From January through August, we make parts for our toys. Then in September we begin final assembly and painting so that they'll all be ready by December 1. Once a week, all of us get together for four hours to work on core parts; the schools let us use their wood shops. Then we refine and finish off our pieces at home."

Jane Sprang, eighty-two, began working at Unity Shoppe shortly after she moved to Santa Barbara from Wisconsin in 1982. "I was widowed, and needed something to do," she said. "I used to work here practically full time, wrapping gifts and putting away knitwear and other items. Now I get here each day at nine in the morning and work until one or two in the afternoon when I go home on the bus." Among hundreds of volunteers, the local RSVP organization honored Jane as its 1999 Volunteer of the Year for her work with Unity Shoppe and a host of other organizations.

Sofie Minzel, eighty-six, has also been a volunteer for Unity Shoppe for over twenty years. She retired from the University of California at Santa Barbara and, shortly thereafter, was encouraged by two friends to volunteer with Unity Shoppe. For the first seventeen years, she worked in the senior services department making sure Unity Shoppe's cadre of knitters had the materials they needed. She'd order supplies, make deliveries to the homebound knitters, pack and check the boxes that were wrapped for delivery. "We knit everything from baby blankets and booties to sweaters and afghans," said Sofie. She volunteered forty hours a week for many, many years. Today, Jane and Sofie work side by side on a somewhat less daunting schedule. They fill requests of those who are home- or hospital-bound. "It could be that someone needs a radio, or a sweater, or a clock," said Jane. "We wrap each item with our beautiful gift wrap and ribbon, and address a name tag. We want their request to look like a lovely gift, not a handout."

Sofie continued, "On Wednesdays, I meet with thirty elderly people at the senior center who get together once a week to have lunch. I visit with them and deliver yarn to the knitters and fabric, buttons and thread to those who make dresses for little children. When I was still driving, I'd deliver yarn and pick up the items that had been knit at individual's homes. Today, I teach our new volunteers everything we do. I live in Arizona half the year now, but return every summer to spend six months helping Unity Shoppe."

Volunteers at Unity Shoppe perform all sorts of tasks. Some stock the grocery store shelves with canned goods and boxed products. Others work in the clothing store, the senior center, or the thrift shop. Like Bruce, many work offsite.

People tell the story of one woman who sewed for Unity Shoppe for twenty-four years. Hallie, as she was known, kept scrapbooks of her work, each page containing a swatch of the fabric she'd used and a full description of the garment she'd made. By the time she was one hundred years old she'd made 976 garments. She told everyone that doing something for the children made her feel she was still useful.

"There's great satisfaction in doing something for others, and in doing a good job," said Bruce. "I'm working with other enthusiastic men. My former boss said he never wanted to do anything when he retired. I'm not quite sure why. He's dead now. Our chief engineer was the same way."

"I like the satisfaction, as well," said Sofie. "I love helping people, and I'm so fortunate to be healthy. Not long ago,

Cottage Hospital wanted me to make a basket for a twelve-year-old girl hospitalized with leukemia. I wondered, 'What would she like in her basket?' and decided on Barbie dolls and clothes. It touched me so to help that little girl."

"You meet so many different people here," added Jane. "They help put things in perspective. You think you've got problems? You always find someone worse off than you are, and they need our help."

How did Unity Shoppe begin? In the early 1900s, two young women, new to Santa Barbara, called a meeting with the local visiting nurses association and associated charities. They wanted to encourage volunteers from the entire community to work together to help people in need. The gifts they made were simple and back then the town was small. But the idea of neighbors helping neighbors in a unified effort flourished, and Unity Shoppe was born. It has thrived for more than seventy years as a volunteer organization without monetary assistance from the city, the county, the federal government or United Way. It's a 501(c)3 organization, so all gifts are tax-deductible. And the whole community pulls together to make it happen.

Today with non-profit organizations assisting the homeless and the needy in almost every community, you merely need to join in. Many churches band together in their efforts to help others. Perhaps, they could be encouraged to expand even further, using Unity Shoppe's example.

Bruce, Jane and Sofie are enjoying their senior years and have similar views on retirement. "Seek until you find what you enjoy," said Sofie, clutching her hands to her heart. "The secret is in not staying home—it's in getting out with other people. Even if you're handicapped in some way, you have to get out."

Jane agrees. "It's good for a person to get out among people. That's how you'll discover what you'd like to do."

Bruce concluded, "I never thought I'd retire because I really loved my work. But then when the government imposed so many regulations, it wasn't fun anymore. I did some consulting and thought, 'Why am I doing this? It's more of the same.'

"Now I have a great life, with no time restrictions. Everyday, I'm doing things I enjoy with people I enjoy."

"That goes for me, too," added Sophie.

"Ditto," said Jane.

A SECOND CHANCE

Leo Neff had no idea when he fibbed about his age and joined the Army National Guard at fifteen, that his life would change so abruptly. Within a year the United States was at war in Korea, and Leo's division was called to active duty. At sixteen, his school days were over.

Later, Leo realized he'd made a big mistake, and was eventually able to finish his high school education by completing the General Education Development (GED) program at the United States Armed Forces Institute. He was grateful he'd had a second chance, and went on to earn both bachelors and masters degrees in fine arts. He taught art in the Dayton, Ohio public schools for thirty-one years.

To stay involved in art when he retired, Leo started a computer graphics home business. To stay involved with teaching, he joined the Retired Teachers' Association (RTA). At one of the first meetings Leo attended, the chairman asked for volunteers to tutor inmates at the county jail. "I hadn't intended to sign up. They sent a clipboard around so that volunteers could jot down their names, but by the time it made its way around the room to me, not a soul had done so. I thought

'I can't let this go back like this', and signed my name. Instantly, I became a tutor."

The Greene County jail is a plain-looking, three-story building in downtown Xenia, Ohio. It houses approximately 160 inmates awaiting trial or transportation to a state prison. On each visit to the jail, a deputy leads Leo and his teammate up the stairs and through two barred, locked doors as he accompanies them to the second-floor day room where they will tutor. He stays with them for the duration of their tutoring.

"My teammate was an experienced tutor," said Leo. "I learned by watching her. At the beginning of the session, and at the end, we give the six inmates a little pep talk. We tell them this is a second chance to finish their high school education, that they have six weeks in which to do it, and that getting their GED will serve them well when they're released. It'll also give the judge and prison staff a positive sign that they are willing to improve and change; that never hurts. Then in between our pep talks, we work individually with each inmate.

"Our students are incarcerated for anything from jumping bond and failure to appear in court to harder crimes like murder, rape, robbery and fraud. We try not to know what they're accused of doing. Most are between eighteen and thirty years old, not really mature or motivated. Many come to GED tutoring just to get out of their cells, but there are others who sincerely want to make a change in their lives. Some want to prove to their families they can get back on the right track. Others realize they've made a mistake and want to correct it.

"One big bruiser of a fellow was convicted of fraud. He was manager of a local company and had apparently forgotten to make a deposit. You could tell he was a born salesman. He wrote a wonderful letter thanking the RTA for helping him. We thought he'd turned the corner, but about nine months later he was back in jail.

"Another inmate, thirty-five years old, was very quiet and meek. To look at him, you'd never think he'd ever muster up the initiative to do much of anything. But he was smart and he got a score of 259 when he took the GED exam. A score of 260 is a perfect score and means the possibility of a four-year college scholarship. We were excited about this man's potential, so the RTA paid the forty-two-dollar fee so that he could take the exam again. The next time he scored 260. We were elated. I hope he's done well."

Every week for eight years, Leo has gone to the jail two days a week. Prior to each session, he and his partner discuss their students and any special circumstances going on that day at the jail. They work with prison personnel, contact county schools to acquire necessary signatures, write letters to appropriate officials, and purchase graduation gifts. To date, Leo has tutored 218 inmates to a successful completion of the GED.

Leo feels that everyone deserves a second chance. "Someone gave me a second chance when I took the GED, and I want to give others the same opportunity. It's very satisfying to think that if any of these students become successful, I've had a part in it."

The Greene County program has won several awards, including the J.C. Penny Award for Public Service and the Governor's Award for Community Service. When it started, it was the first such program in the state. Now there are several others initiatives across Ohio using their model.

If you're interested in starting a similar endeavor in your town, Leo suggests you contact the General Education Development office in your state capitol to determine the need in your community. If you have a vocational school nearby, check with them because they may already be involved. If you do go ahead and start a tutoring program, you'll need a sponsoring organization like the RTA to provide a platform from which to operate.

At sixty-eight, Leo says retirement is not exactly what he and his wife, Mary Anne, had imagined. Instead of taking it easy, they both have separate small companies, and find they don't have nearly as much time for travel and leisure as they'd anticipated. Still, they've managed five trips to Europe.

"Is retirement supposed to be that you stop and not be of service to others?" Leo asked. "I don't think so. I feel if we stop, we're dead. Each of us should have an avocation—something we love to do. I love to teach. If you're not sure what you love to do, think about the things you do when you're alone that you find enjoyable. How can you expand on those? Start dreaming again, and follow your dream. Don't lose sight of it, and when the time is right, do it.

"I've known retirees who scatter their efforts every which way. They're so excited with their newfound freedom. That may be interesting, and entertaining. But it doesn't last. For life to be truly meaningful, you need to find the thing that really grabs you. That's what brings passion and excitement to life. It may take some time until you find it, but it's worth persevering until you do. There's no substitute for having discovered that one, special thing you love to do."

Martin Luther King is credited with saying it, and Leo buys into it:

"An individual hasn't started living until he can rise about the narrow confines of his individualistic concerns to the broader concerns of all humanity."

AN ARTIST, AT LAST!

"I'd wanted to be an artist my whole life," said LeAnn Word of Odessa, Florida. "I wanted to talk to artists, be around artists, and do what artists do. I wanted to smell the paint, and have my own brushes, and know everything there was to know about art. But like most of us, I had other priorities. I didn't have the time or money when I was younger—kids, husband, work. So I decided that rather than take just any job, I'd look for jobs that required artistic effort, as a compromise."

For several years, LeAnn taught crafts—first at a hospital, later at a crafts supply shop." It helped, but LeAnn was still not an artist. Someday, she hoped to illustrate the children's stories she'd written. She'd written eleven over the years, including "The Frog in the Mouse House." But they were still in the filing cabinet, waiting to be taken out again into the light of day. "I didn't even know how to draw a mouse," she said, laughing.

LeAnn was in her mid-fifties when a neighbor decided to take calligraphy classes and asked if she'd like to go with her. From that first lesson, LeAnn was "home." She loved the class, and since her teacher also taught art, she signed up for her water color class, as well. "It was heaven," she exclaimed. Then she signed up for oils. And acrylics. And colored pencils. And charcoals. Before she knew it, LeAnn had enrolled simultaneously in seven courses offered by two nearby senior centers.

LeAnn was beginning to feel like an artist. Morning classes started at 9:00 or 10:00 A.M. After breakfast with her husband, Robert, LeAnn would pack her lunch and take off for the day. Usually, twelve to fourteeen seniors attended a class. They'd paint, talk, have a mid-morning snack, paint and talk some more, and break for lunch.

The next class would start around 1:30 P.M. and another group of twelve to fourteen would show up for lessons. Four or five were regulars at these three-hour sessions, like LeAnn. "It gets to be a way of life. Thank heavens my husband was so supportive. He knew how important this was for me. I went to classes all day, everyday, Monday through Friday, for nine years!

"By the time I was sixty-four, I decided I could cut back on my classes. I began thinking about how I could use what I'd learned. I'd always loved teaching crafts. Maybe I could teach art."

LeAnn began teaching at the Odessa Community Center two and a half years ago, and at another community center nearby. Each private lesson she offers is three hours in length, and she teaches whatever the student wants to learn in whatever medium they prefer. She charges a small fee for the lessons, and advertises in the community newspaper. All her lessons have been private. "Students are so open to ideas, and all can learn. I don't use the word 'talent.' I believe in 'development.' With lots and lots of practice, everyone can develop.

"I'm building my credentials at this point. I sell hand-painted greeting cards to friends, and the Life Enrichment Senior Center in Tampa, one of the places where I took lessons, sells note cards at local fairs and craft shows to raise funds." The cards show the scanned images of paintings of its art students. LeAnn's paintings are among them.

"I've sold paintings, but every painting I've ever sold I ended up wanting back. I don't paint for other people, I paint for myself."

LeAnn's advice to other would-be artists? "You need to take that first step. Almost every community or senior center offers art lessons, and usually the lessons are quite affordable. Jump in! Try things! Some folks may not want to try total immersion as I did, but it is certainly a fast way to get you started and help you sort out what you like to do. My favorite medium is water color. To me, it's the easiest, but maybe its because I learned water color first. Take as many lessons as you can and buy the best equipment you can afford. Persistence, persistence! Keep at it and you'll be surprised at what you'll be able to do."

"What are your thoughts about retirement?" I asked.

"Isn't it wonderful?" LeAnn replied. "My children are grown, I don't have to work anymore, life is easier, and I don't have to fight for anything—money to pay the bills or keep the car running or get the kids to school. Life is a struggle for all of us. Now it's so much less work, and so much more fun. It's the best time of my life!

"Everyone should have a passion, particularly in retirement. I don't care if its stacking marbles. All of us need to do something we love. I like teaching people something they didn't know before. Who knows? They might be enriched by it. It might change their lives. I'd like that. And I like to give them a laugh or two.

"There are too many people at home sitting in their rocking chairs," LeAnn continued. "I worry about them. We never know how long we have. Those folks need to get out of the house, be with people, and find something wonderful they enjoy. Use their time on this earth fully! I have! After dreaming about it all my life, I'm finally an artist."

A RETAIL ADVENTURE

"We looked at a clock store, a truck rental business, a hardware store, and a greeting card shop. The broker tried to get us interested in restaurants. But we decided on Groff's Wallpaper because it was a new business located on a major thoroughfare, and we could imagine opportunities for innovation," Gwen said. Although they knew nothing about what they were getting themselves into, Gwen and Jake Jolliff embarked on an eighteen-year career in retailing.

Jake retired as vice president of a fiber and yarn business in Asheville, North Carolina; Gwen had been a homemaker and mother. They decided to move to Raleigh to be closer to their grown children, although they weren't sure what they'd do when they got there. But the idea of owning a mom-and-pop business was appealing.

"We didn't know a thing about retailing," said Jake. "Thank heavens, we inherited our employees. We'd have been lost without them. How do you go about buying wallpaper? Which patterns will sell? How do you price it? What kind of systems do we need to put in place? What kind of bookkeeping? We did it all by trial and error."

Gwen did the buying. She had a background in commercial art and started out just buying what appealed to her. "Soon I found that if you listen to your customers, they'll tell you what they want. And then you can make better buying decisions," Gwen said. "Of course, I didn't know a thing about pricing either. If the pattern didn't sell at $8.99, we'd price it at $7.99, and then at $6.99. Sometimes I priced it higher, put it in another part of the store, and it would sell immediately.

"That's another thing we learned," Gwen continued. "You can't keep your stock in the same place all the time. You need to move the patterns around from shelf to shelf, or from one section of the store to another, to add interest and appeal."

Groff's Wallpaper was unique because they carried more than one thousand patterns on the premises. Imagine the inventory they had with all those patterns in stock, multiple rolls of each! Displayed next to each of the patterns were 4"x4" samples cut for customers to take at will. "If they wanted larger samples, we would give them those, too," Gwen said.

"We kept the original owner's name for the store because he had just purchased a full page ad in the phone book. We wanted to take advantage of a year's worth of free advertising." The store was open from 9:30 to 5:30, Monday through Saturday, and Friday until 9 :00. They had no walk-in business because they were located on a busy highway. But their uniqueness drove the business—they were a large "destination store" devoted only to wallpaper. No paint. No fabrics. Just wallpaper, in quantity.

They started with three thousand square feet of floor space, and as stores next to them vacated, expanded to six thousand square feet. In addition to the sales floor and "kiddie korner" of toys, they had an office, a budget room/classroom, and a storage room. Twice a month, they held free wallpapering classes for up to fifty learners.

Jake took care of the business end of things. He devised a labeling system with codes that provided all the basic information needed for tracking and bookkeeping—cost, retail price, pattern number, vendor, date received, purchase order number.

Computers didn't seem necessary. Instead, they used the "green book," a soft cover, three-pronged notebook—the kind you'd find at any drug store. The notebook contained a swatch of each pattern with pertinent information next to it. Searching through swatches on the page was so much easier than looking through line after line of numbers. And so much faster.

Gwen and Jake were devoted to their four employees, all of whom had prior decorating experience. They paid high wages, set up a pension plan, and gave employees one to two weeks vacation a year. "Two of our employees were with us for twelve years. We had no turnover unless an employee's spouse moved the family out of the area," Jake remarked.

They never had a year without making a good profit. When the boulevard in front of the store was torn up to construct a major highway, Gwen and Jake expected a loss. But it never came.

"And when Home Depot opened right up the street, we were sure it would affect us," Gwen said. "But it didn't. They didn't carry the variety or volume of wallpaper we did, and their employees were not as knowledgeable about decorating."

The fun part of the business was different for each of them. Jake loved the challenge of doing something new and different; Gwen loved it all. A stay-at-home mom and homemaker until her late fifties, the business gave Gwen an opportunity to spread her wings and draw upon her background in art left dormant so many years before.

Jake said, "Twice a year we went to trade shows. There were seminars where dealers from across the country would learn from each other. We made some wonderful friends. And vendors told us our product selection, business knowledge, customer relations and employee dedication combined to make us their outstanding account. That was satisfying."

At the start of their eighteenth year in business, the property owner informed them he planned to demolish their store and modernize the shopping center. A large retail mall was being built next to them and the property value had increased dramatically. He bought out their lease, and they agreed to vacate in forty-five days. Eighteen years of business ended very quickly.

Each employee was given a generous separation package. The pattern books were sold to decorators and vendors. Their display tables and racks went to an existing dealer in another town. They held a huge sale and got rid of half their stock. The rest was donated to Habitat for Humanity.

I interviewed Gwen and Jake eight days after they had locked the doors. They were still recovering from all the work of closing shop. Now in their seventies, they know they'll do something else but right now, they need time for rest and recreation.

What advice would they give others who might want to do something similar? "Talk to people in retail to find out what it's really like," Gwen suggested. "If you can't give it the time that's needed, don't do it. A business ties you down—you need to be there. We said we'd go away once a month if only for a long weekend. But that didn't work. There were always business reasons for being at the store."

Jake continued. "Just about everyone who goes into business goes in under-funded. Try not to do that. You really do need a financial cushion when you start. And then be really careful with your spending. Last, if you treat your people well, you needn't have the usual retail turnover."

Gwen and Jake feel that owning the business stretched them. "I learned that I have a lot more physical stamina than I thought," Gwen said. "It was a wonderful opportunity to get out there and do something. I didn't want to be one of those older women who do nothing but baby-sit their grandchildren, as nice as my grandchildren are."

Jake continued. "We learned a lot about each other. We learned how to handle our disagreements, and appreciate each other's strengths. We made some really good choices together."

"What about moving to Florida?" I asked.

They laughed. "The people we knew who moved to Florida have all died," Jake asserted. "They weren't using their mind, their bodies, their wits. We're not sure what we'll be doing next, but we won't be moving to Florida to play golf."

"So many people focus on "senior moment" memory lapses, and their aches and pains," concluded Gwen. "When I hear someone saying they've forgotten, or that this or that hurts, I tell them to shush. All they are doing is reinforcing the negative, making it more real. We don't want to focus on aches and pains. We want to remain challenged and busy and learning new things. We don't know what it is, but we've got another new project just around the bend."

MONTY'S JOY JUICE®

"Today's a great day!" exclaimed Monty Justice, seventy-five, of Louisville, Kentucky, as we began our discussion of his new life. "We just got our first international order."

Retired from a metals manufacturing company in 1985 after thirty-four years, Monty had no idea what he'd do in retirement. In fact, he slept for the first two weeks after he left work. Then he got a call from Charles Dawson, a nationally recognized rosarian and gold medal award recipient who founded the Louisville Rose Society. Charles had a thriving business growing greenhouse roses and caring for other people's rose gardens, and he'd been Monty's friend and mentor for a long time.

"I know you don't want to retire," Charles said, "so I've got just the right job for you—rose care. You don't have to know a thing about it. I'll teach you everything I know." Charles had more business activities than he could handle, so he asked Monty to take over the year-round care of six of his customers' rose gardens—planting, feeding, spraying, pruning, and winterizing. In effect, Charles gave Monty a starter business.

"It was fun," Monty said. "Years before, I'd begun experimenting with liquid fertilizer mixtures to enhance the growth of my roses, and they were looking pretty good. I wanted other people's roses to look as good as mine. I accepted Charles' offer and continued experimenting on these six rose gardens, amending soil and applying my plant food just as I had on my own.

"One concoction I came up with grew great roses, but killed all the grass close by. Another time, the roses turned out beautifully, but seventy-five of the plants died during the second winter. The fertilizer had lowered the *ph*—it had become too acidic. But through trial and error, I eventually got a formula that worked. It was so exciting. We called it 'Monty's Joy Juice.'"

The results were spectacular: fuller bushes, larger blooms with more intense color, and healthier plants. Word spread about Monty's good results and by the third season he had ten additional gardens to tend, but sadly, his most helpful friend, Charlie Dawson, died.

Through word of mouth, more and more customers learned of Monty and came on board. "I took pride in helping others find the joy and beauty of roses," Monty said. "We hired high school and college kids to help me.

"Within a couple of years I had over one hundred gardens to tend. My family and I made it an official business."

Monty's Rose Care, LLC was formed in 1991. "My son-in-law had acquired a complete grounding in rose care while working for me part-time during graduate school. We became partners. He takes care of all the business aspects as well as the maintenance of the gardens. I teach, go out with our work crews, buy roses to install, price the work, do the billing and try to solve the unusual rose problems. It's not a perfect science. Every problem is an opportunity to learn."

By this time, Monty had been hired by some of the famous horse farmers around Lexington to consult with them and install their roses. He had developed three distinct formulas: an all-purpose growth formula for outdoors, a seed starter for indoor potted plants, and another to develop more roots and enhance the blooms. He mixed them in his garage, storing them in plastic milk jugs, and began using these food-grade compounds on everything. His materials are completely safe and non-toxic.

Soon Monty realized the stuff he was making was good, and it should be marketed. Urged by family and friends to start a big business, Monty told them he was too old for that. But they persisted. "We'll do everything you don't want to do. All you have to do is talk," they said.

"That sounded like a good deal to me, so I'd go to flower and garden shows all over the area, talk to people, and give them free samples of Monty's Joy Juice. We hired an experienced marketing person, obtained a trademark, and a local bottling company got us out of the garage. Our first professional-looking bottles and packaging came out in June 1998. At the same time, a respected local columnist wrote a terrific article about us for the newspaper. It brought over 1,100 inquiries about our juice. That did it—our second business was up and running.

"We got lots of free publicity through feature articles in the newspaper, and our products were sold on Home Shopping Network. A Louisville TV station asked me to give rose growing tips during the spring planting and growing season. Although I wasn't to advertise Monty's Joy Juice on the show, the publicity alone brought our products to the public's attention. At times, we felt in over our heads. It was a lot to take on in two short years.

"Now we sell mostly to nurseries and garden stores through distributor relationships. With increased usage in the grower and agricultural markets here in the US and now with our international presence, the future is bright for Monty's plant food. I know I've been given a gift that was providential and I'm grateful to God for His blessing."

Not long ago, a novice rose grower with only nine bushes started using Monty's Joy Juice on her plants every week for two months, following his directions precisely. She wanted to enter the Louisville Rose Show. Not only did she enter, her rose was judged best of seven hundred entries! "In all my years of experience, I've never seen a novice rose grower win Queen of Show," Monty said proudly.

People have told of Monty's Joy Juice enhancing the blooms of impatiens, improving blackberry yields, producing sweeter tomatoes, monster cabbages, and early fruiting of banana trees. They even use it on their African violets, orchids and *bonzai*.

"What's great about all this is that I'm pursuing what I love. I'm doing this with my family. We're all excited about the business, and we love knowing our product has brought joy to many diverse growers while ensuring the environment is completely safe."

"How do you feel about retirement?" I asked.

"I wish I'd retired earlier. It's too short. Retirement is an opportunity to do the things you couldn't do before. It doesn't mean doing nothing. If you've done a good job of financial planning, you can do whatever you choose."

"Monty, when we began our interview you said that you had had no idea what you were going to do when you first retired. A friend opened the door for you. What advice would you give to others who don't know what they want to do?" I asked.

"Look around. Talk to people. If you don't have a passion of your own, start investigating other people's passions. Partner with others. Work on whatever you're doing until you do it very, very well. Then give it away. Even if you sell it, the secret is in doing for others, not keeping it to yourself. The pleasure is in the giving."

MUSIC FOR MINORS

Picture a petite, tow-headed Mary Poppins. In her colorful ankle-length skirts and petticoats, looking every bit like the Mother Goose, Mother Nature, and Mother Earth she plays at schools, British-born Margaret More has found her niche. Her degree in theatre and dance, and experiences in early childhood education and professional storytelling, are perfect credentials for being a docent with Music for Minors (MfM).

MfM began twenty-five years ago when music was dropped from the public elementary school curriculum in California. Its highly trained volunteers bring music, dance, and performance to students in thirty-four elementary schools in the San Francisco Bay area. "Each week I'm fortunate enough to teach two kindergarten classes in one school, a second/third grade in another school, and two after-school classes," said Margaret.

When she saw an MfM recruitment flyer at the library, she knew the job was tailor-made for her. Volunteers must have an extensive background in music and in working with children, and once accepted into the program, must attend MfM's fifty-five hours of training. "The first thing we learned was how to pack as much as possible into a thirty-minute session without ever being hurried. We have lesson plans timed to the minute, but no one suspects. No matter what we're doing—starting, ending, even when we're passing out instruments—we're doing it musically. The children are so happy to see us. We try hard to create a 'what's she going to do next?' atmosphere.

"The programs incorporate music from various cultures, so the children are learning on many levels. MfM has a wonderful resource center filled with puppets, tambourines, dancing poles, instruments, classical recordings, holiday theme items, and international props. An introduction to Orff instruments is included in our training. I love using Orff xylophones, metallophones and glockenspiels because removal of tone bars that are unnecessary for a given song maximizes a child's success in playing it."

This past year, Margaret made sixty penguin costumes, with tails, for her kindergartners (and herself, of course.) "We had a penguin party, invited the parents, and in the end the parents and children danced together. The children are so used to seeing me in costume that one day when I wore just a skirt and blouse, a little boy asked, 'Who are you today, Mrs. More?'

"Next year, I'll be the liaison between the school administrators at MfM at my grandson's school, in addition to the classes I teach. With all the preparation needed prior to classes, our personal travel time to and from schools, trips to the resource center, our monthly meetings, and the classes themselves, you can see that being a docent requires a real commitment. But I love it. I have a million ideas about what I want to do. I *love* music—it's my passion!"

There's that word again . . . passion. "Suppose you don't have a passion, Margaret? What does a person do then?" I asked.

"Your work on this planet is to live your passion, so you have to find it. You have to put yourself in a situation where you can find it. Ask yourself—'if there were no-holds-barred, no limits financially or in any other way, what would I want to be doing?' You're never too old to do something you dream about! In America, you can do anything you want. There is no limit. You have to stop that critical voice inside that says you're too old or incapable. Anything worth doing is worth doing poorly until you learn to do it better. So try things, and find the very best teachers to help you. Find others who will support you. Stay away from the ones who don't."

"What other recommendations do you have for retirement?" I asked.

"I'd start on this before I retired. Begin the training, the research or whatever you'll need to begin your dream now, so you can just step into it when you retire. Enroll in a class that will challenge you and get your imagination flowing. I've noticed that when people have identified so strongly with their jobs and done nothing else, their whole world ceases when they retire. Some people need fallow time to discover who they are. When my husband, David, retired from Nortel, he didn't know what he'd do. He needed fallow time. After awhile, he got involved with Habitat for Humanity and now he builds houses three days a week and loves it."

"How would someone else with a passion for music start a program like MfM elsewhere in the country?" I asked.

"First, find others who are passionate about music—contact local music groups, church choirs, put up 'Music Lovers Wanted' notices in the library. Gather a core group of three or four people.

"Second, call the Music for Minors office in Los Altos. I'm sure we'd be delighted to support a new group, and show them what we do."

Margaret says she receives incredible joy from participating in the MfM program. "To see those little guys light up, come alive, is super satisfaction. Parents tell me their children talk so excitedly about their music. Teachers who at first were reluctant to give up a half hour to music, come enthusiastically on board when they see the value of what we're doing.

"I love dreaming up things, getting creative. I'm dyslexic and had a terrible time in school. Because I've never forgotten how hard learning was, I find ways to make learning easy. I'm a

Capricorn, a ham—all my life I've wanted to be outrageous. Now, at sixty-three, I feel okay being outrageous. It makes no difference to me what people say or think. When I go to heaven, I'm going to ask to sing four-part harmony all by myself. Till then, this will do very well."

FOXFIRE

In the quietly elegant colonial town of Middleburg, Virginia, an idea was born for a product that could change the way people build houses all over the world. Bringing the centuries-old, time-honored adobe tradition into the twenty-first century, Stephen Keiley, founder and CEO of Foxfire Associates, has designed and built a block. That's right. A soil-and-cement block. "We saw a massive housing problem worldwide and figured out a way to deal with it," Steve said.

"Bricks and block need mortar to hold them together and to compensate for the lack of uniformity in size. With mortar, brick or block walls are made to look uniform, and rows are made to look even. But mortar is expensive. Professional bricklayers are expensive." Steve and his associates at Foxfire saw an opportunity.

They designed TerraBuilt® blocks—blocks that hold together with a simple tongue and groove design. More important, the size of each block produced by their modest hydraulic block maker is within 1/64 of an inch of every other block it produces. In the construction trade, this uniformity is called being "dimensionally accurate." It's almost unheard of, and a very big

197

deal. Their simple machine, powered by an eight-horsepower engine, can be easily towed from one building site to another. It can pop out a new compressed earth block every 15 seconds— a block that doesn't need mortar.

"No mortar means no bricklayers. It means stronger houses because mortar is the weakest element in a block house. It means houses that can be built by unskilled labor, or volunteers. It means savings of time and money. And many, many unskilled people could be put to work building houses in developing countries."

Ever the entrepreneur, Steve formed Foxfire at age sixty to explore possible solutions to social problems in developing countries. "It's not a retirement business. Its just another one of my enterprises," he said. "I can't relate to retirement: working for an employer, finally leaving with my gold watch and going off to play golf. Years ago I thought that's what I wanted. I got my Harvard MBA and joined the corporate world. But about that time John Lindsey, mayor of New York, was asking for young managers, leaders, MBAs to come work with him in New York. He said something like 'I want people to help! New York needs you!' And I was cocky enough to think he actually meant me!" Steve laughed.

"I went to work for John Lindsey and found out what heady stuff it can be being faced with intense challenge. Right then and there, I realized I was made to take a risk, to take on a big challenge. I loved going for it. I loved seeing the problem, working with others to come up with the solution, and making things happen. At sixty-three I haven't changed—maybe slowed down a little in my approach—but I haven't changed, because this is what I love."

"But a block? Why invent a block? Are you an engineer?" I asked.

"No," Steve replied, "but when I've been in other countries and people point out interesting problems, my mind automatically starts working on solutions. I don't know why that is, but I've always been that way. I see opportunities everywhere I go. I've done a lot of work in developing countries.

"Years ago, while in Sri Lanka, I learned that a soon-to-be built hydroelectric dam would wipe out millions of tons of timber. That would have been a tragedy in a country with no oil or coal, in which 90 percent of the people use wood to cook in their homes. But transporting low value, non-commercial grade timber out of the path of the dam was not economically viable. As I began thinking about the problem, I realized the solution was to convert the wood to high value charcoal on-site, doing it as a highly profitable commercial venture. The government embraced the idea, we set up a company, and today thousands of people have jobs producing tens of thousands of tons of charcoal. The country has a new, more convenient form of household cooking fuel, as well as a high-grade industrial fuel. Later, we took the idea to Malawi in Africa."

Steve and his colleagues see TerraBuilt blocks as a potential solution for affordable housing, and they are poised to introduce their product to other countries. "Right now we're negotiating in Mexico, Central and South America, and with China. We can have an enormous impact on millions of unskilled people by providing them with construction jobs and with homes. And that makes this a meaningful challenge for all of us."

"Will this be your life's work?" I asked.

"No, I'm smart enough to know that good entrepreneurs do not make good managers. Once we have large-scale contracts with clients and need to produce blocks by the thousands, we will need to spin off this technology into another company. When I see that company running well, and I no longer need to be heavily involved, I'll be free to pursue something new for Foxfire. I don't know what those ventures will be, but there are always problems in the world to be solved."

"What advice would you give to other entrepreneurs?" I asked.

"At this age, I think you need to have a burning passion to do something that's beyond yourself. Otherwise, it would be easy to run out of steam. You need to have a background that will support your venture. I couldn't now be trying to negotiate with governments of other nations if I hadn't done this before and didn't know the ropes. You've got to have good health." Steve smiled. "And you need a spouse who's tolerant of your workaholism. But if you like a challenge, have a tolerance for risk, have a dream of helping others, and a group of supporters and collaborators, I say go for it. If not now, when?"

SCHOLARSHIPS FOR ALL

In 1987, a prominent resident of Paragould, Arkansas, who had no children of her own, told her accountant she wanted to give $15,000 to establish a scholarship fund for the children of her community. Within a year, another woman who'd read about the gift in the newspaper, gave $25,000. Members of the Chamber of Commerce established a fund. "And then a Paragould businesswoman bequeathed an amazing seven hundred fifty thousand dollars to the cause!" said Evangeline Cothren, seventy-seven. "That was more than enough to endow what we named the Greene County Scholarship Fund."

Now in its sixteenth year of operation, the endowment annually pays out scholarships of varying amounts to graduates of all of Greene County's five high schools and to home-schooled seniors planning to attend an accredited college or university, regardless of their grade point average or test scores. In a county of only thirty-six thousand citizens, the idea has so caught on that twenty-three other local citizens have established endowments, as well. Today, the fund totals over $1.5 million.

In addition, one-time gifts of about $100,000 are given annually by individuals and organizations.

Evangeline, a teacher in Greene County's Tech High School for thirty years, businesswoman and president of the Chamber of Commerce at the time of the initial donations, was a logical choice to head up the scholarship committee. She and the members of the group work throughout the year on scholarship business, although their most active period is from January through June.

Each January, the scholarship application forms are sent to high school guidance counselors. By late March, the students who are applying have returned their completed applications to the scholarship fund. Then for the next six weeks, Evangeline and members of the grants committee meet every other day to decide who will receive which scholarships, and for what amounts.

"Some donors have specific students in mind for their scholarships; others have specific qualifying criteria—for example, the recipient must be someone who will be studying economics, or who will be attending their college alma mater. We check with the guidance counselors to see if students are receiving scholarships from other sources. If so, we're likely to award less money to that student and more to someone not receiving other funds. Eventually, we sort out who gets what. This year, 253 seniors will receive a total of 353 scholarships, totaling $171,640 and averaging about $700 per student.

"We notify the students of their scholarships by letter, inviting them to attend the awards ceremony that is held during the first week of May. A great deal of time is spent organizing the evening presentation. We publicize the ceremony in the newspapers, and invitations go out to the recipients and their parents, guidance counselors, donors, and sponsoring organizations in the community. Well over one thousand people attend, so we rent the big new building at the fairgrounds—the only place in town large enough to accommodate all of us. One of our banks graciously pays for the rental of the building. A local print shop donates the printing of the programs, and inmates from the local jail clean the hall, assemble the chairs, set up the stage, and afterwards, fold and store the chairs, and clean up. With each recipient receiving their scholarship(s) individually, it's a long and happy ceremony.

"Once the big event has been held, we update our database. Then in August and September, when we receive proof of the recipients' enrollment, we send scholarship checks to their colleges and universities."

To keep the fund in the public consciousness, the committee provides news of their activities to both of Paragould's newspapers, and the *Jonesboro Sun*. Committee members speak at church groups, civic organizations and women's clubs. "You just never know when the word is going to fall on fertile soil," said Evangeline, "and another person will want to establish a scholarship. Even with the market as it has been in recent years, we've never had to hold a bake sale or fund raising drive."

As we sat and talked in Evangeline's downtown office, I commented on how ironic it was that all three of the initial contributors to the scholarship fund had no children of their own, and how admirable and unusual it is for a group of citizens to band together to award scholarships to a community's college-bound high school seniors. "It must make you feel proud to be associated with such an endeavor."

"It's satisfying to me," Evangeline replied. "I've had a good life and this helps me feel like I'm paying back. And it's fun. I've learned all sorts of things being a part of this effort."

Evangeline offers the following suggestions for those who might want to start a scholarship fund in their town:

1. Get a group together who believe in the project.
2. Devise a plan for making it happen. And then find ways to learn from others. Here in Arkansas, the Walton Family Charitable Foundation brings consultants to Little Rock every month who hold seminars for people involved in philanthropic work. We've attended those, learned a lot, and made many contacts. You may find similar

foundations in your state that focus on philanthropy, education or community enrichment and development.

3. Apply for 501(c)3 tax status for your endowment, or find a foundation already operating that will act in your behalf and invest your money. This is what we've done. The Arkansas Community Foundation serves as our Board of Directors and charges us a fee for their services, but it's worth it to us not to be involved in all the paperwork required by the IRS. You'll need that charitable designation so that donations can be tax-deductible.

4. Make publicity an ongoing priority. Every time we're in the news, we tell our story all over again so that people understand and support what we're doing. I think our publicity has helped citizens have confidence in us and that's why we get money so easily. We've been in the news regularly for sixteen years.

5. You'll need to be willing to make a real time commitment to your scholarship fund. Year-round, I probably spend a third to half of my time on it. Between the scholarship fund and my involvement in the courthouse preservation project and the Retired Teachers' Association, I'm as busy as I've ever been. And that's the way I like it. I wouldn't want to sit and twiddle my thumbs. I wouldn't be happy.

"What advice would you offer those about to retire?" I asked.

"Be thinking about what you want to do and how you can help those around you," Evangeline replied. "We need to be giving others a hand along the way. In the process, you'll find you're learning and growing every day, that your mind is engaged, and that you're truly involved in life. Isn't that what we all want?"

MILL CREEK FARM

There were horse pastures on either side of me. Down the road was the barn, and seventeen barking dogs of every size and description, tails wagging, running my way. I slowed the car to a crawl and inched the rest of the way to the barn so I wouldn't hit any of them. They didn't jump on me when I got out of the car—just encircled me, happily waiting to be acknowledged. And there was Peter Gregory. "Welcome to Mill Creek Farm," he said.

Years ago, when Peter and Mary Gregory were attending the University of London, they had often visited an equine sanctuary on weekends. "Maybe someday we can do this," they thought. Peter's career in the hotel business took them all over the world, but they never lost the dream. Finally, with the children grown and gone and enough money for their new venture, they purchased 245 acres of lush, rolling open land in Northern Florida.

Peter and Mary wanted to make a place where old retired and abused horses could live out their days in a peaceful, caring setting. They built their house first. Then it took a year to get the property ready to accommodate their vision. They spent $150,000 in fencing to enclose the 22 pastures. Three deep-water wells were drilled and miles of pipe laid underground to supply fresh water to the troughs in each pasture. Open shelters were built to shield the horses from Florida's hot summer sun and the occasional storm. Finally, Mill Creek Farm, a Retirement Home for Horses, was ready for business.

"We informed the University of Florida veterinary school and the Humane Society, and word spread," Peter said. "Our first horse was actually a tiny pony named Trigger. The ropes around his neck had been tied so tightly they were imbedded in his flesh. With tender care, the wounds eventually healed and Trigger learned not to be quite so fearful of people." Soon another pony arrived, named Joseph. Peter smiled. "Trigger and Joseph were inseparable and roamed the property freely, often following us around. Joseph finally died of old age. Trigger died of a broken heart soon after."

Nowadays Peter and Mary have 110 horses, their limit. "We want every horse to have two acres of grazing land," Peter said. "Each pasture contains five or six horses." Some are disfigured from abuse, some are blind, and many are scarred. Six have no teeth and have to be fed a special diet of mash five times a day. But all live the good life until they die.

"Five years after we began, we formed a not-for-profit Florida corporation—Retirement Home for Horses, Inc.—to which we transferred all the land and its improvements. Our house was included, but we have lifetime tenancy. Contributions to the farm are tax-deductible. It costs approximately $1,000 in direct expenses to care for each horse. But that figure nearly doubles when you include overhead expenses such as salaries for our two employees, insurance, utilities, office supplies, repairs and maintenance. The farm is open to the public on Saturdays only. Admission is two carrots. The entire funding for the farm is based on the goodwill of others."

What advice would the Gregorys give to others wanting to help animals? First, you have to be devoted to them. "Animals don't know the difference between Christmas, the fourth of July, or Thanksgiving," Peter said. "Their care must go on 365 days a year.

"Second, animals can't be left alone. There are 'round the clock matters needing to be taken care of in a large operation like ours. We work from sun up until late in the night. Several times a day, I make the rounds, checking the condition of each horse, the fences, and the pastures. Do the horses appear well? Is anyone sick? Has any horse died? They are old, and we have one death a month, on average. Are any fences broken? And of course, all the animals need to be fed, groomed, and receive their medication. You can't take off for a day at the beach unless you can afford to pay your staff for that privilege.

"Third," added Peter, "set up a board of directors. Our board consists of two veterinarians, an animal activist, a fund-raiser, and Mary and me. We rely on our board members' advice and assistance.

"Fourth, enlist volunteers. Every Thursday and Saturday, our wonderful group of volunteers come to groom the horses. Other volunteers help us with the maintenance of the farm. Even our veterinarians and our farrier provide their services free or at reduced rates," he said.

Now seventy-four and seventy, respectively, Peter and Mary have been concerned about Mill Creek Farm continuing on after they're gone. A perpetual conservation easement on the land now ensures that, for all time, the land can only be used as an equine sanctuary—a major accomplishment and a big relief to Peter and Mary.

"We love what we do," Mary said.

Peter agreed. "Every day is a new adventure. Along with our horses, we have five pot-bellied pigs, a one-thousand-pound hog, four cats, and our seventeen dogs. When one of our animals dies it's like losing one of our family. But we tell ourselves they've had five or six happy years they wouldn't have had otherwise. We love them all; they've learned to love us. And we love having dedicated ourselves to something we feel is important."

Retirement for the Gregorys is about love.

MUSIC AND MUSINGS
WITH THE NSO

For fifty years Ken Pasmanick was the first bassoonist with the National Symphony Orchestra (NSO). In a life that most of us only dream about, he performed with Leonard Bernstein, Yehudi Menuhin, Pierre Boulez, Jasha Heifitz, Leopold Stakowski, Bruno Walter, and Mstislav Rostropovich, and traveled the world from Milan to Montivideo, Madrid to Moscow, Paris to Peru. When home in Washington, he rehearsed each morning, taught in his studio in the afternoon, rushed upstairs for dinner with his wife and children and then changed into tails and hurried off to perform with the symphony. He was used to hearing applause four nights a week. "Playing with the symphony and the Washington Opera and Washington Ballet as well, I was Mr. Bassoon in Washington, D.C., for many years," Ken said. "When I retired at age seventy-two, it all stopped—rehearsals, teaching, performances, applause.

"The first few months of retirement were exhilarating—the freedom, the lack of schedule, the quiet, and the time to enjoy

nature which I love. But a few months later I found myself
unhappy and at loose ends. I suddenly didn't know who I was
anymore. I missed the life I'd known and my professional identity.
I didn't think life in retirement had much to offer without the
symphony and my immersion in high-level music making and
attendant activities. In this culture of ours that defines who we are
by what we do, I felt like a non-person.

"Then one day, a light went on. I realized that rather than
being a non-person, I'd been a total human being before I ever
saw a bassoon, and I was a total human being now. The question
was, 'What was I going to do to make my life meaningful and
enjoyable once again, involved with people?' I felt isolated.

"I walk a lot for exercise, forty-five minutes to an hour every
day. One day I walked past the Methodist Home, a retirement
community. 'There must be people there who'd love to hear
my music,' I thought. I met with the activities director and she
said they'd be honored to hear me play. So a few weeks later I
spent an hour with the residents of the Methodist Home, talking
about my career, interspersed with playing tunes."

Not long after, the activities director had a visit from Rosa
Weinstein, the founder of a mobile university that brings classes
to seniors in retirement and nursing homes. Himmelfarb Mobile
University, named after the foundation that supports it and run
under the auspices of the Jewish Social Service Agency of
Metropolitan Washington, is directed by Rosa. Retired military,
educators, musicians, engineers and the like present offerings
to elders on subjects as diverse as ethics and politics, opera,
American history, the "New Deal," famous persons, and lost
tribes. Rosa asked Ken to join them.

For the past few years, Ken has presented "Music and
Musings with the NSO" at nursing homes, assisted living
facilities, senior centers, retirement villages, and the Jewish
community centers in Washington, Maryland and Virginia.
He's performed for AARPs Widowed Persons program, and
for American University's Institute for Learning in
Retirement.

"It's enjoyable," Ken said. "Usually I start by playing 'It Might As Well Be Spring.' Then, in a group of thirty-five or so, there'll be a couple of live wires who start asking questions, and that gets the ball rolling. We talk. I tell them about life in the NSO. Then I'll go on to 'There'll Never Be Another You,' or maybe 'What Kind of Fool Am I?' And we talk some more. It's not always the same. But when I leave, I feel I've paid back by sharing the pleasures of a successful career. I'm useful, and I'm enjoying the tactile experience of holding that maple wood and the immediate connection with my innermost feelings. I feel like I've done a good deed. I've brought joy, comfort, nostalgia. I find that I reach people; that people are touched by what and how I'm playing, and the commonality of emotions that we all share as humans.

"I miss playing chamber music. But to do that I played and rehearsed several hours each day. I don't want to practice like that anymore. There's a whole world out there. I've found that if I play three hours a week I can sustain my embouchure (facial muscles and placement of the lips), my diaphragm muscles and manual dexterity, and that's all the time I'm willing to put into practice now."

"Himmelfarb Mobile University is a great idea. What would you tell others who'd like to do something like Himmelfarb?" I asked.

"First, you've got to want to be with people; to give to people, for the pleasure you get from giving. When you perform for money, a certain degree of satisfaction involves your pay. When you're volunteering, you're doing it only for the pleasure of giving. One discovers the pleasure of giving in seeing appreciation, surprise and delight on people's faces. You want the thrill and pleasure of seeing that response from other people—so much better than money.

"Second, it doesn't have to be your profession that you're talking about. It can be your hobby. There's a woman who talks about Hollywood, another who talks about anthropology, another who talks about opera. None of them had careers in those areas. All of us are creative and need to exercise that part of our being. All these people have put together very interesting talks."

Rosa Weinstein says its helpful to have a platform from which to operate. The endorsement of the Himmelfarb Foundation and the Jewish Social Service Agency lends legitimacy to the project. The foundation provides generous annual funds to cover a stipend to Rosa for coordinating the program, and to pay for volunteer mileage, expenses, etc.

"So, five years into retirement, what do you think of it now?" I asked.

"I love retirement," Ken exclaimed. "It's a wonderful opportunity to put focus on how fortunate we are to be alive! What is it you've always wanted to do? Or, what is it you've been doing and would like to share with others? Now's the time to do it.

"You have to face it. You can go into deep isolation and withdraw from life. Or you can use your time of being free by doing something wonderful."

Above Ken's desk in his studio is a yellow Post-It stuck to the bookcase. On it he's written "LIFE—Be In It!"

CONCLUSION

"LIFE. Be in it." Ken Pasmanick's note to himself succinctly states what all the men and women portrayed in *Starting Over* have demonstrated. You've read their stories of focus, passion and accomplishment; of reinventing life after sixty in ways that bring immense satisfaction and enjoyment. Some of them volunteer, some have businesses, but all are using their skills and talents in new and different settings. The Japanese have a word for it—*ikigai*—which means finding significance and purpose in later life.

That sense of purpose didn't come easily for some. They hadn't had a plan, exactly, but thought they'd enjoy golfing, boating, gardening, maybe a little consulting—kind of taking it easy, dabbling in this and that. After all, isn't that what we worked for all these years? Fun at first, they discovered that dabbling gave them a degree of short-term satisfaction but no fire-in- the-belly excitement; no challenge, no reason for getting up in the morning. Eventually, they sought something with more 'punch.'

Even for those of us who had an interesting and meaningful endeavor lined up before we left the workplace, retirement is still a major life transition and adjustment. It's not just a matter of closing one door and opening another, like moving from one house to the next. It's more like moving from one house to no house; like moving to an open field. A house has structure, with an address—an identity. Each room has a purpose, a way to get in and go out. But the open field of retirement is free form. Until we make it into a house, with new purpose and identity, that lack of structure can be scary and quite unsettling. At least, that's how I found it.

Many people have asked about my own *Starting Over*. During my last few weeks of employment, I was positively giddy with anticipation. But when Friday, November 9, 2001 arrived, it felt like I was jumping off a cliff. After thirty years in offices, hotels, conference centers and classrooms around the world, I walked out the door, got in my car, and drove away from the corporate world forever. Left behind was the structure of a well-formed life, a community of co-workers I'd been a part of for years, a world of goals and deadlines, celebrations and frustrations, and a place to go. Ahead of me was . . . space. Free-flowing time. Boundary-less expanse.

I knew what I wanted to do. I'd begun *Starting Over* at a lovely resort in the Ojai Valley in California a month before I retired. It was an inspiring and beautiful location for reflection, dreaming, and getting clear about the purpose and framework for the book. I felt a real sense of accomplishment as I arrived back at my office a week later, and during the next few weeks, conducted my first interview.

Then November 9th was here. Luncheons, cakes, presents, hugs and it was over.

Going to bed that first Sunday night without setting an alarm was delicious. My circadian rhythms have never adjusted to 5:00 A.M. wake-ups.

I awoke at 8:00 Monday morning and sat in the sun room, breakfast tray on my lap, watching the *Today Show* until 10:00. The phone rang throughout the morning—friends calling with congratulations, wanting to take me to lunch. Hours were spent on the phone and later, at the computer. I was finally beginning my project in earnest, and was anxious to dive in.

Life was so exciting. Each morning as I awoke, I'd lie in bed for a few minutes, relishing the joy of knowing the day was mine; not my employer's, not my children's. "Thank you, Lord, for this day of freedom—this day to do whatever I want." It felt like the exhilaration I've experienced upon awakening for the first time in Paris or London or some other exotic location, impatient to step outside to discover and enjoy.

It was warm for November and the sun was shining. The holidays were approaching, with Christmas shopping to do, and visits with my grown children and their families. Most of all, there was the book. It was the first thing I thought about each morning and the last thing at night.

Every free moment was happily devoted to it. Each time I learned of likely story candidates, I'd call and introduce myself, tell them about the project, and ask if they'd like to be a part of it. Almost everyone said "Yes." Each "find" was cause for celebration.

January's cold and darkness didn't seem to depress me the way it usually does. While busy tracking down story leads, interviewing, and writing, I was making arrangements for a trip to Florida for sun and several interviews. Applying my skills to this new, exciting territory of writing a book, finding a publisher, and then promoting it was all virgin territory for me. I had lots to learn and much to do, and I felt more alive than I had in years.

Feeling alive. Being passionately absorbed in something. That's what retirement should be about. The people featured in this book spoke as one about feeling alive, the need to find a passion, the joy of having problems to solve and risks to take, barriers to overcome and goals to achieve. Life, for them, is intoxicating. They're in it on their own terms, loving every minute of it. And now I was in it on my own terms, too. Could anything be more wonderful?

Joseph Campbell, the noted author and scholar of comparative mythology, said in his conversations with Bill Moyers on public television that we're all seeking the experience of being alive, so that we actually *feel the rapture of it.* No longer distracted with raising a family and earning a living, we can follow our bliss and dare to go for the rapture as we reinvent ourselves in our later years. When else have we the opportunity, day after day, week after week, to do so? We have the choice of actually doing that word—retiring—to the safety and comfort of the tried and true, with time to dawdle, or we can aim for the rapture of a new adventure and that feeling of being truly alive.

The men and women portrayed in *Starting Over* have chosen the latter, and they and I offer this advice to you as you begin your own over-60 *Starting Over:*

Step One: FIND A PASSION. While you're still working, figure out what new and meaningful adventure you'd like to embark upon in retirement, and have it ready to step into when you leave the workplace. If you haven't any idea what you'd like to do, here's a way to begin considering your options. Start by thinking seriously about two things: your skills, and the things you feel passionate about.

First, your skills. You've spent a lifetime acquiring them. Which do you most enjoy using? What do you do particularly well? What has brought you compliments from others? Probably those areas in which you excel will come readily to mind. As they do, make a brief list. Try to think of at least eight skills. Your family and colleagues at work can help if you get stumped.

Second, think of the things you feel passionate about. Passions cover both ends of the spectrum: those things that make our hearts sing (we'll say they're at the green end of the spectrum) and those things in life we find particularly upsetting (we'll say they're at the red end.) Either end of the spectrum will work. This time, make two lists: "Things I Love" and "Things That Make My Blood Boil." Think broadly. An example follows:

Thing's Mary Loves	Things That Make Mary's Blood Boil
dogs and cats	spoiled brats
jazz live performances	rape, sexual abuse
singing jazz	voter apathy
children	graffiti
politics	violent movies, songs
travel	child abuse
animal rescue/foster care	rude, disrespectful behavior
group discussion	gridlock
learning	
public speaking	

Now, pick one item from either of your passion lists. Then consider how your skills might complement that area of passion. For example, "Mary" has spent years speaking to groups. She enjoys the interaction with others and is a skillful speaker. She's also passionate about the welfare of animals and children. Can you think of ways she could use her speaking skills to battle animal or child abuse?

On behalf of animal rescue groups, Mary might visit schools and teach responsible animal handling. She might teach the same to new pet owners. Maybe work in fund-raising. If she decided to focus on abused adults or children, instead, she might teach classes on parenting to new mothers and fathers, or speak to community groups about the needs of the abused.

The point is to pick something from your passion lists and investigate the organizations and activities that support it. Then jump in. It's not likely that you'll figure out what you want to do by standing on the sidelines. Dick Bierly got involved in environmental issues when he became alarmed with the plans developers had for his community (the red end of the continuum for Dick.) With neighbors, he joined in to address the issue. That led him to becoming involved in even larger environmental issues relating to the entire North Carolina coastline, and now he lobbies and testifies before the North Carolina legislature. Dick says real satisfaction doesn't come from sticking your toe in the water from the shore. A sense of connection and meaning only happens when we jump in and become immersed in it.

Step Two: **WHATEVER YOU DECIDE TO DO, GIVE TO OTHERS.** The fastest way to give your life meaning is to do something for someone else. It sounds so trite. Yet every person featured in *Starting Over* is providing something for someone else. Through services graciously provided and/or products lovingly made, the men and women featured in the book have found the secret. Herb McKittrick mused, "I wonder why I never got involved in giving earlier in my life." Mel Nowland said, "The only true joy is the joy of giving." Through giving, these folks are aware that their efforts matter and thus, their lives. As you'll discover, finding a passion that somehow enriches the lives of others will, in fact, enrich your own life the most.

Step Three: **DEVELOP NEW FRIENDSHIPS.** Expect your workplace friendships to change when you retire and if work was the source of most of your relationships, it's time to begin cultivating new ones. In the story of Mitzvah Clowns, Mike Turk discussed how important friends are at this time of life. Once you leave the workplace, you'll be missing the stimulation of daily social interaction and the warmth of those workplace connections. It's easy for depression to take hold unless you find a way to have regular meaningful contact. Whether single or married, become involved in community activities that will provide new friendship possibilities. Research in the field of aging is clear: those with close relationships are healthier and live longer than those without. Intimacy—that is, one person with whom to share life's daily ups and downs— is the key. It doesn't need to be a spouse, or even someone of the opposite sex. It just needs to be someone who cares, daily. Pets bring warmth and closeness to our lives, and that wonderful, unconditional love. But for intimacy, we need a special friend.

So get out of the house, smile, and chit-chat with those whom you encounter. A new friend could be around the corner.

Step Four: BEGIN NOW. The stories of *Starting Over* demonstrate forty different directions for you to consider that are growth-filled and purposeful, and if you combine aspects from one story with another, there are many more. Think of all those possibilities—animals, children, the elderly, arts, crafts, computers, music, writing, teaching, conservation, ESL, community beautification, civic activism, historic preservation, cooking, business, toy making, farming, mental health, inn keeping, museums, international aid, philanthropy, and support of those in crisis. Which stories resonate with you? What areas spark your interest? To which are you drawn?

Choose an area that has appeal, from the book or elsewhere, and begin to investigate. The advice of Margaret More comes to mind: "Your mission in this lifetime is to figure out your passion, and do it." Look on the Internet. Read your local newspaper. Consider your lists. How can you help? Who can you call? What can you learn? Where can you show up?

Starting Over is meant to inspire and inform you of myriad directions you might consider in reinventing your life. I hope you've been intrigued by the activities, advice and ideas offered. *What you do at this stage of life will either enhance your years, or shorten them dramatically.* Plan to live to be 100 because it widens your lens and helps you think bigger. Think BIG. BIG. You might actually make it to 100, and imagine all that you'll accomplish. Decide on a path and go for it. If the first path you choose isn't the right one, pick another. Begin again.

If you begin now to find a passion, give to others, and form new friendships as you contemplate the years ahead, you'll be well on your way to shaping an exciting and meaningful new adventure. The men and women depicted in the book, and I, happily proclaim this to be the best time of life. It can be that for you, as well.

Finally, to stay focused now and throughout the years ahead, periodically ask yourself these four essential questions:

1. **What is the purpose of my life now?**
2. **What will make my life in retirement truly meaningful?**
3. **What will make me feel I'm contributing to our universe?**
4. **Fifteen years from now when I look back on what I've accomplished, will I be pleased or have regrets?**

Joseph Campbell's words bear repeating—*"We're all seeking the experience of being alive so that we can actually feel the rapture of it."*

I wish you a rapturous reinvented life.

PK
Leesburg, VA
May 2003